MIND-BENDING
MAZES

TEST YOUR BRAIN AND INGENUITY WITH 80 CHALLENGING MAZES

This edition published by Parragon Books Ltd in 2017

Parragon Inc.
440 Park Avenue South, 13th Floor
New York, NY 10016
www.parragon.com

Copyright © Parragon Books Ltd 2017
Individual puzzles created by Any Puzzle Media Ltd

ISBN 978-1-4748-8132-6

Printed in China

INSTRUCTIONS

Welcome to this collection of 80 mind-boggling varied mazes!

HOW TO SOLVE
To solve each maze, simply find the route from the in arrow, at the top or left-hand side, down or across to the out arrow, at the bottom or right-hand side.

All of the mazes will be challenging, to test even the most experienced puzzler, and they increase in difficulty as you work through the book. Some might take seconds to complete but others might take much longer, depending on how quickly you find the right path.

There is only one solution to each maze, which is given at the back of the book if you are truly puzzled.

TYPES OF MAZE
This book contains dozens of visually different mazes, but most of them stick to the basic rules of simply following an elaborate path from the entrance to the exit. A few, however, have a simple extra how-to-solve instruction:

Bridge Mazes
In these puzzles you can now cross over and under the bridges.

Multi-level Mazes
These puzzles consist of multiple linked mazes. When you reach a number, you can either carry on over it *or* if you wish you can change level by continuing from the same number in one of the other mazes on the same page.

Warp Mazes
When you reach a letter, you can either carry on over it *or* if you wish you can warp to the same letter elsewhere on that row, and then carry on from there.

1. CLASSIC MAZE

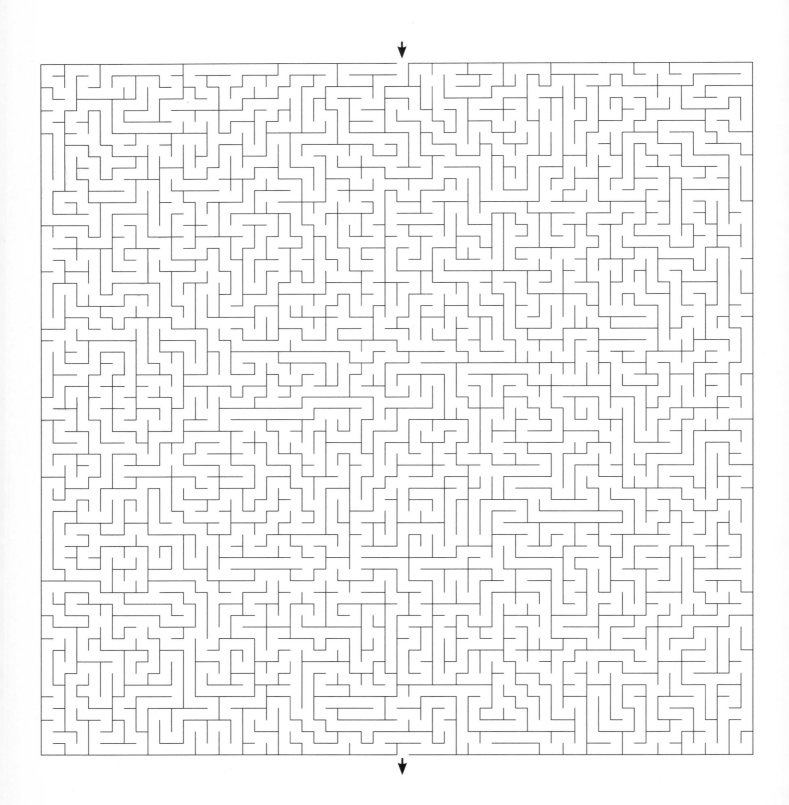

2. PENTAGONAL MAZE

3. GAP MAZE

4. RIPPLE MAZE

5. TRIANGULAR MAZE

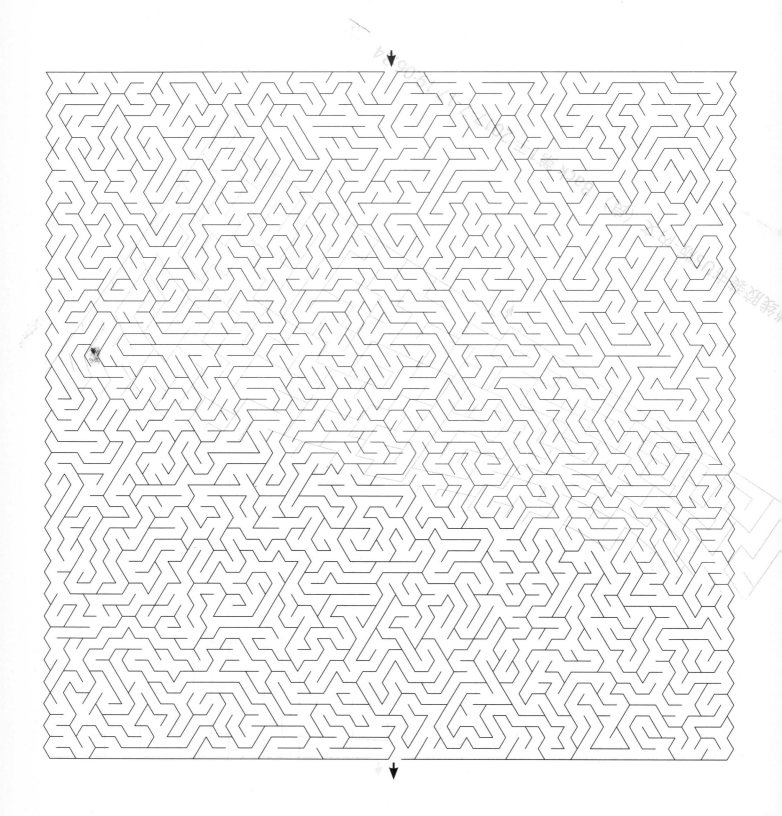

6. CIRCULAR MAZE

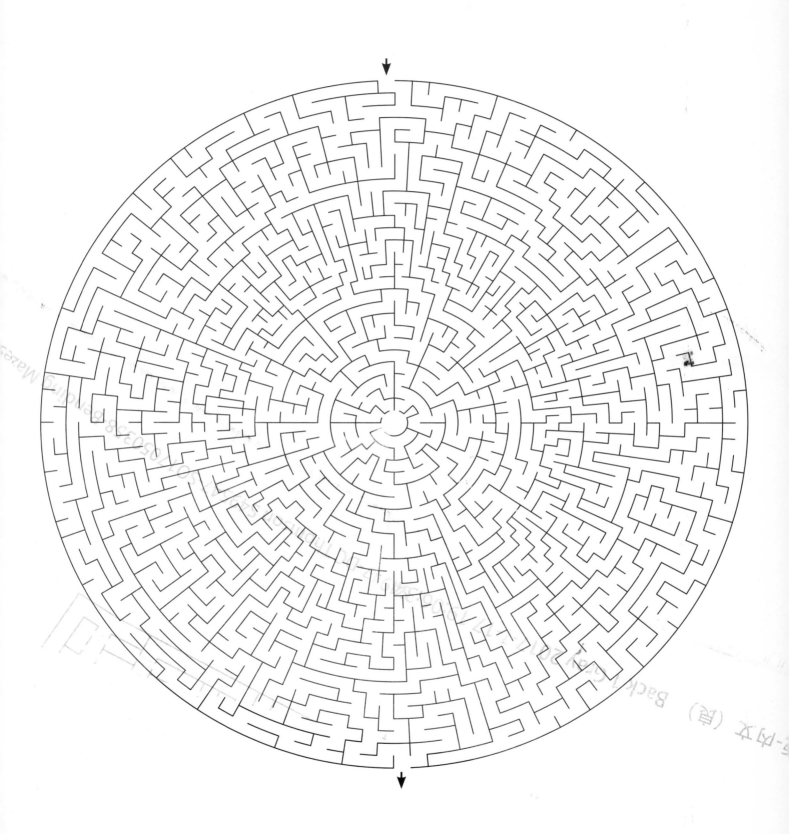

7. BRIDGE MAZE

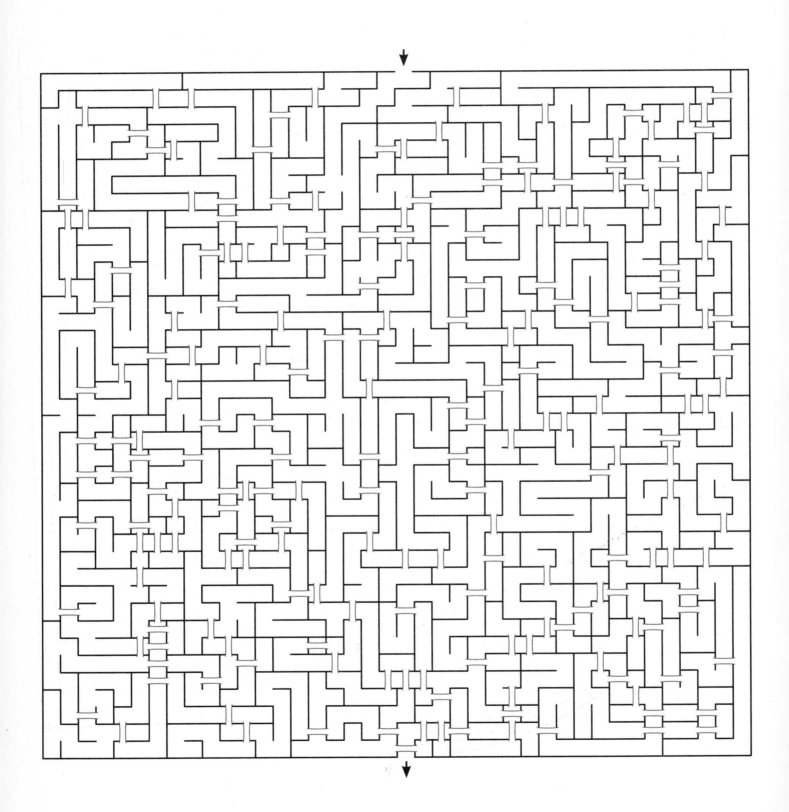

8. ROOMS MAZE

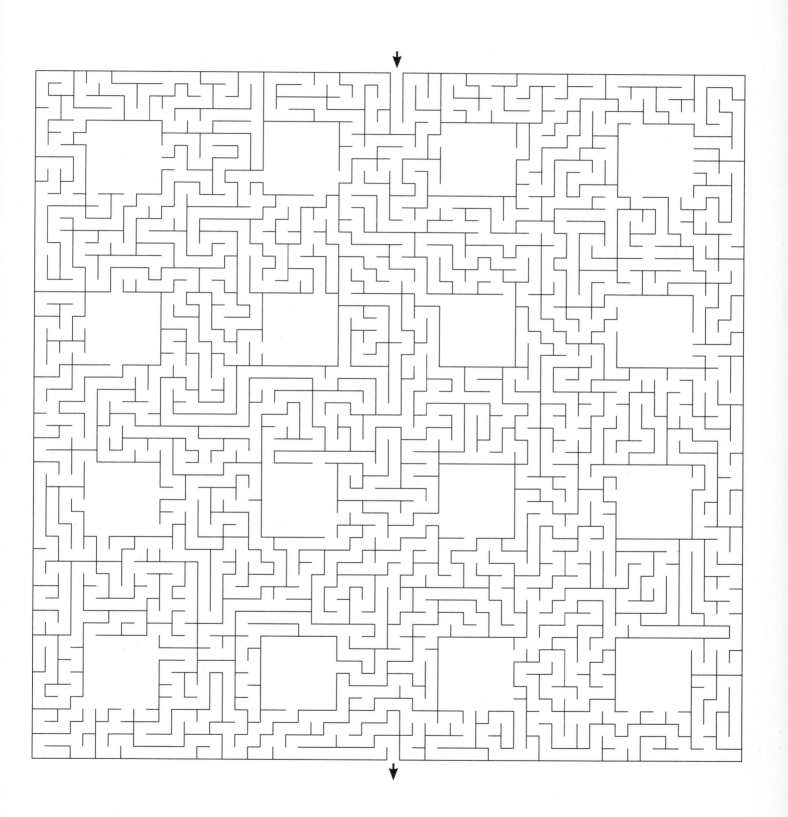

9. TWISTED MAZE

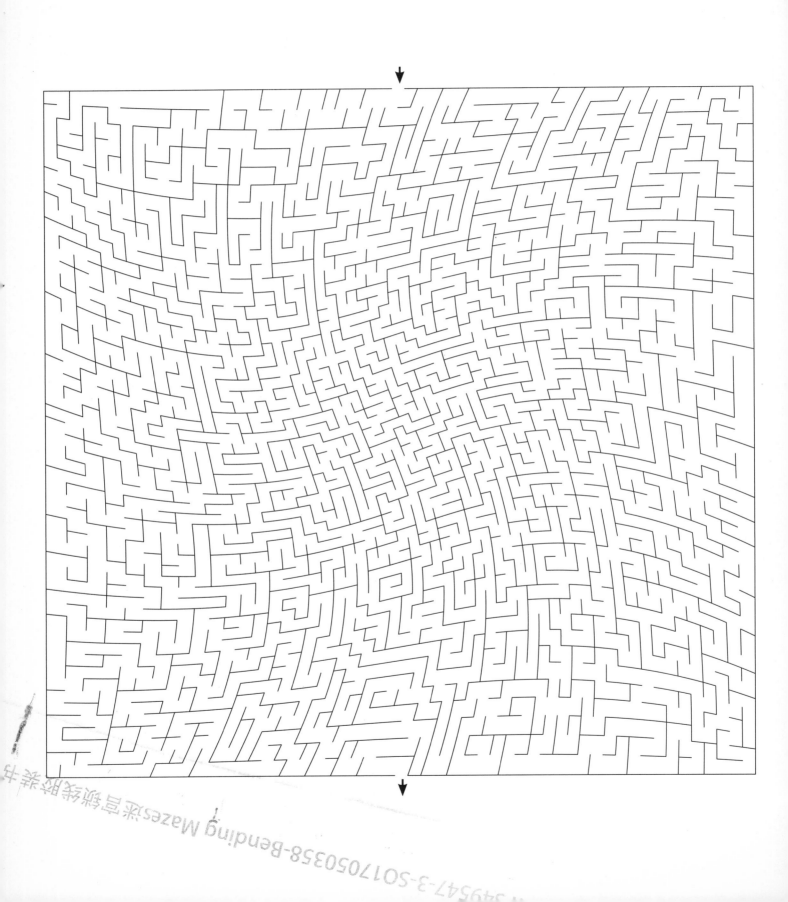

10. OCTAGONAL MAZE

11. X-SHAPED MAZE

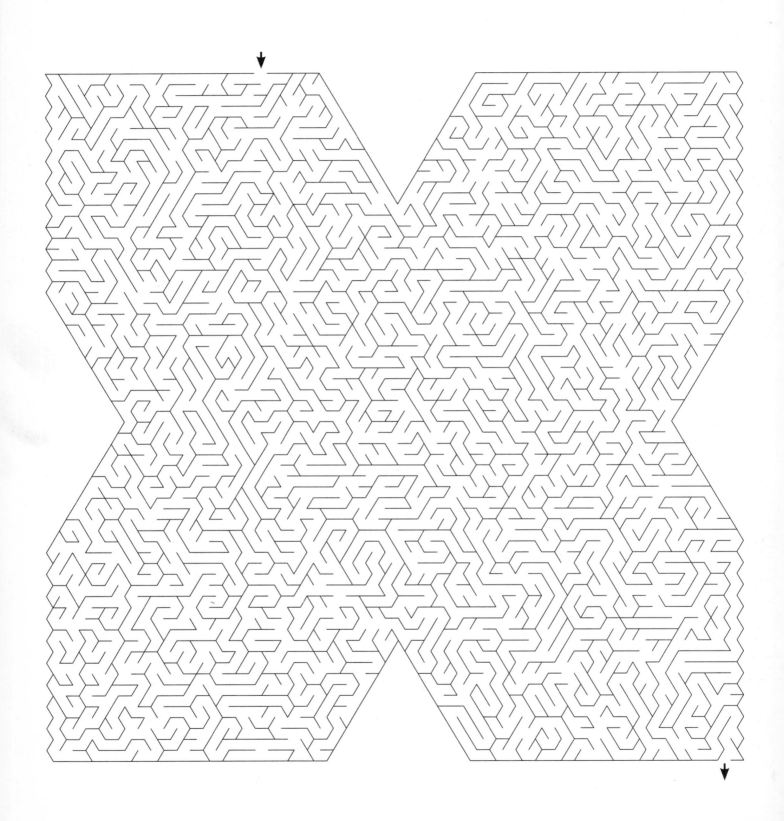

12. CLASSIC MAZE

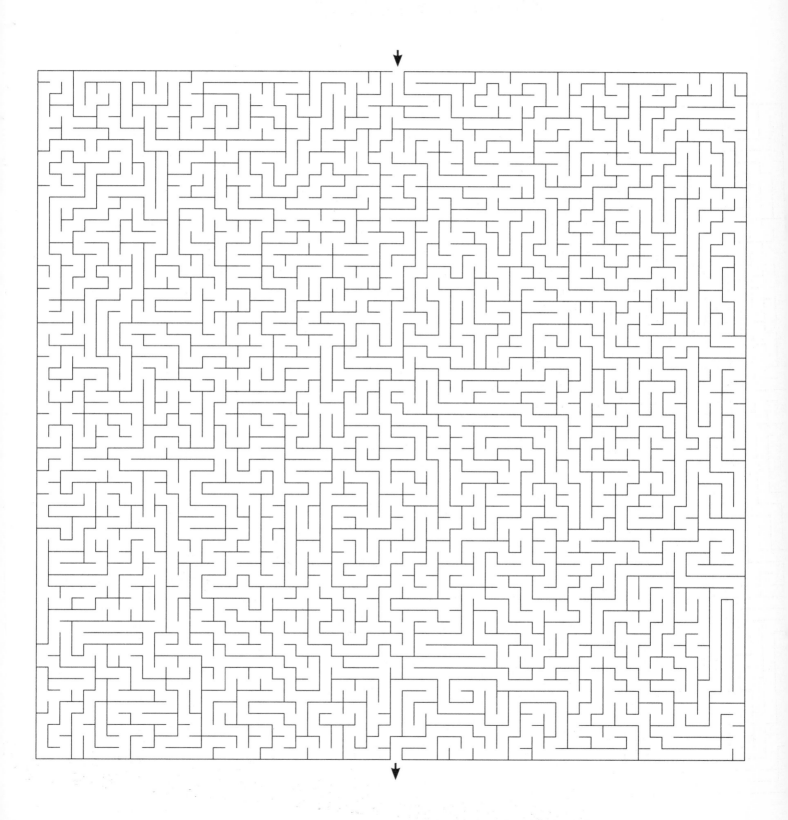

13. INFLATED BRIDGE MAZE

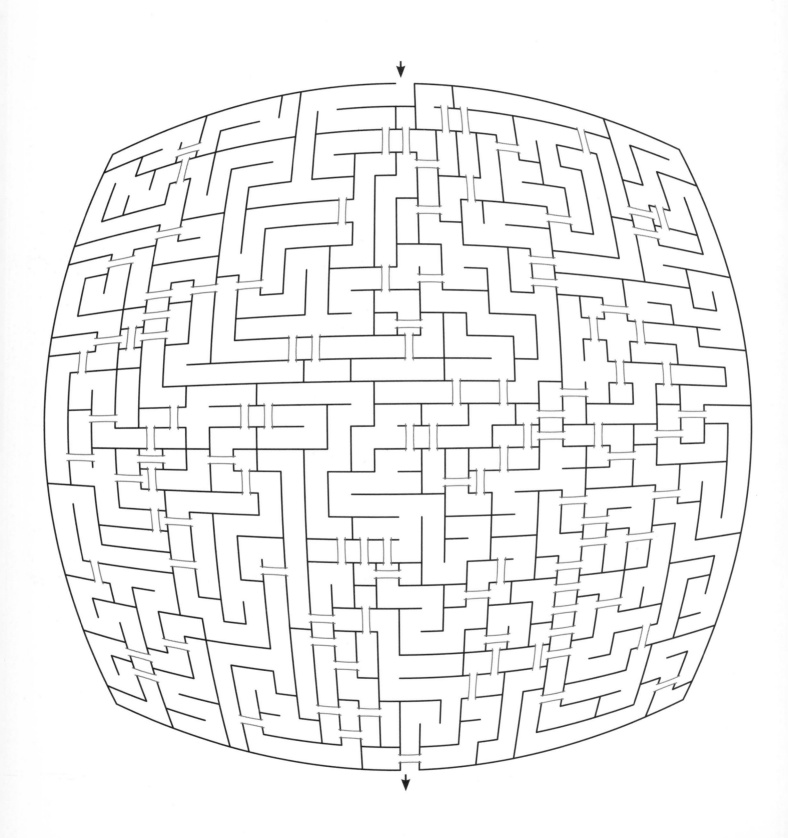

14. CORRIDORS MAZE

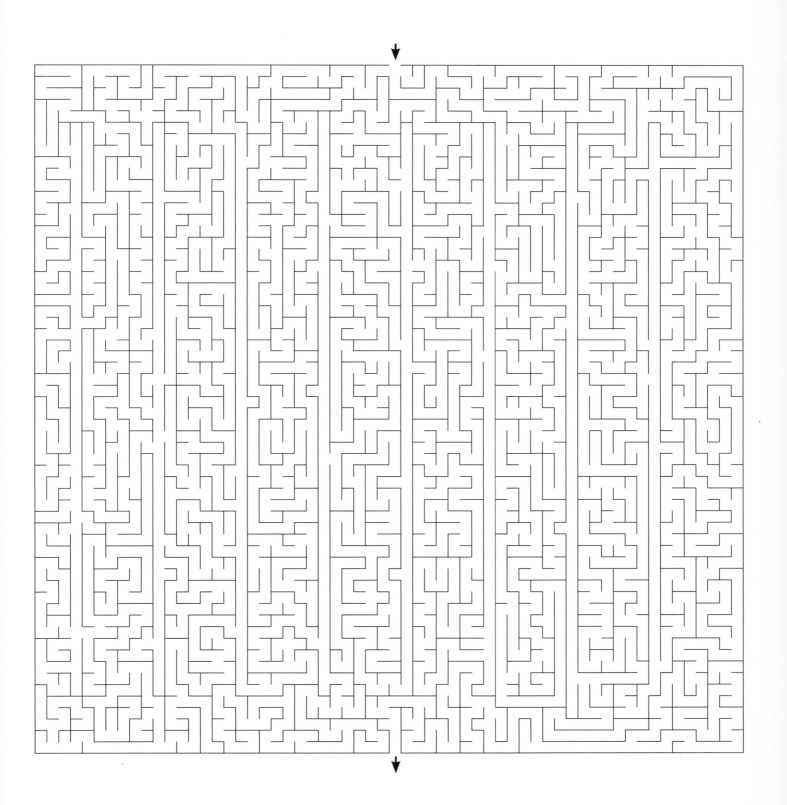

15. CURVING MAZE

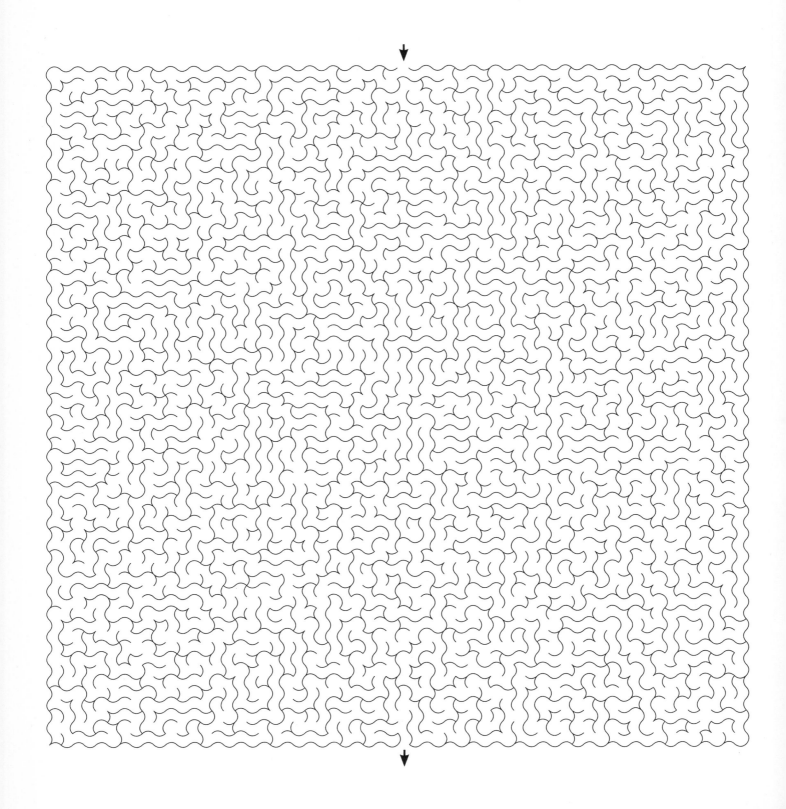

16. DIAMOND MAZE

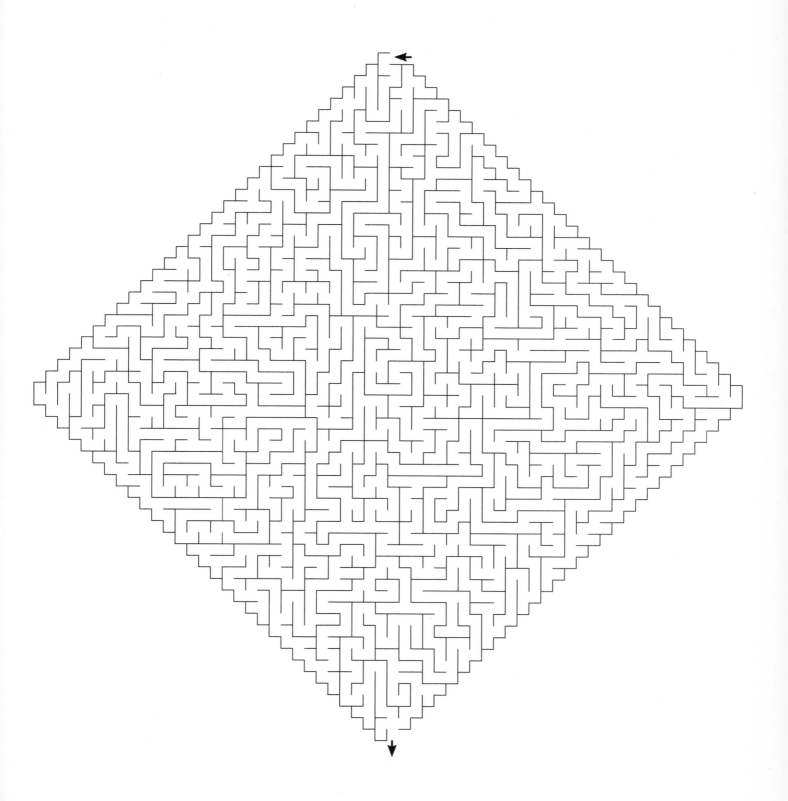

17. CIRCULAR MAZE

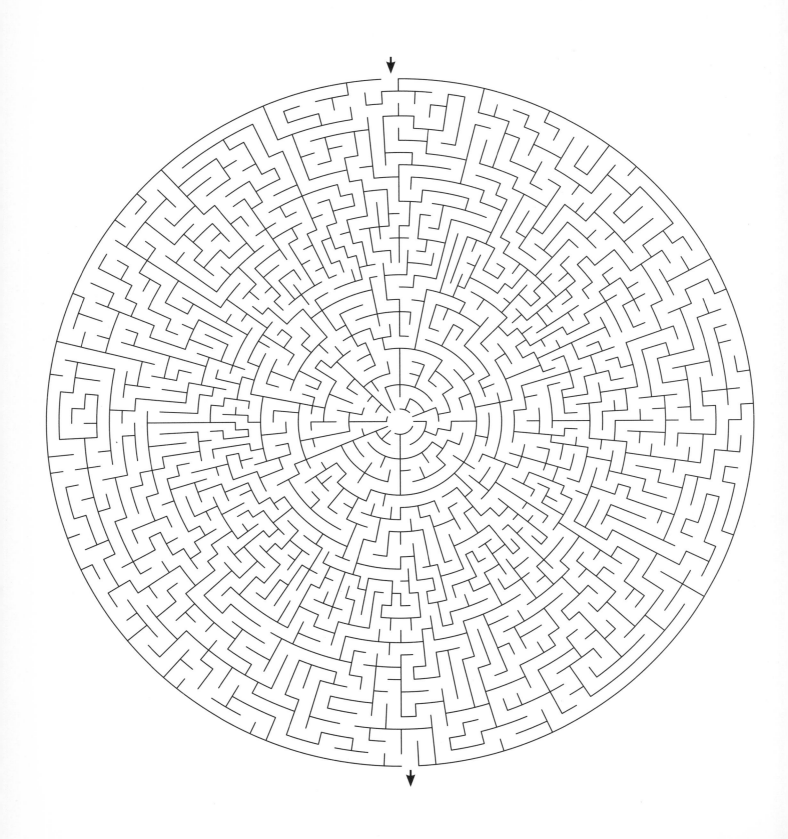

18. CLASSIC MAZE

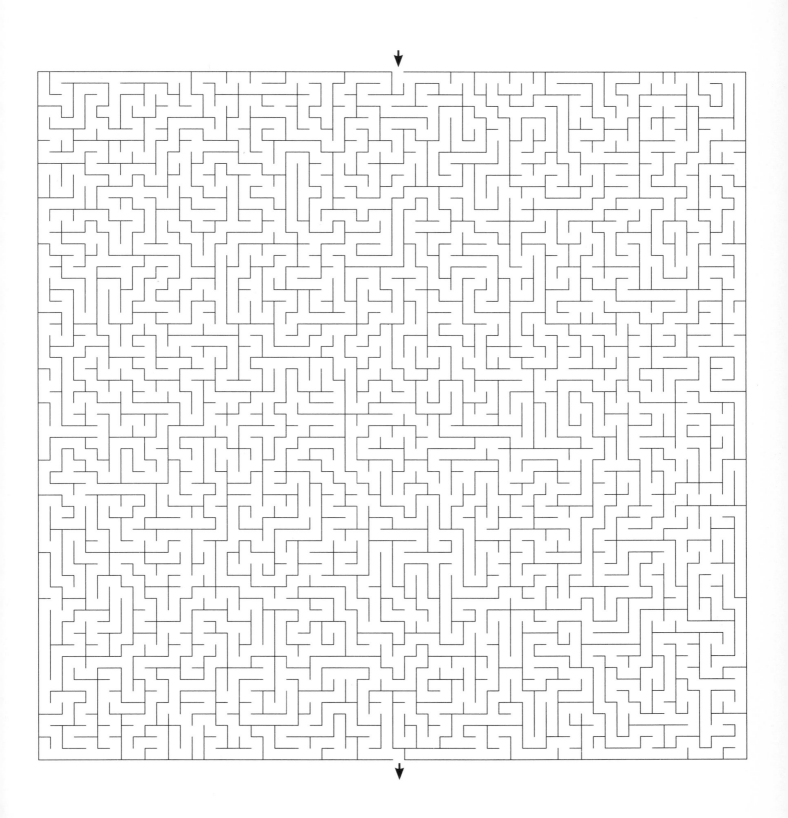

19. GAP MAZE

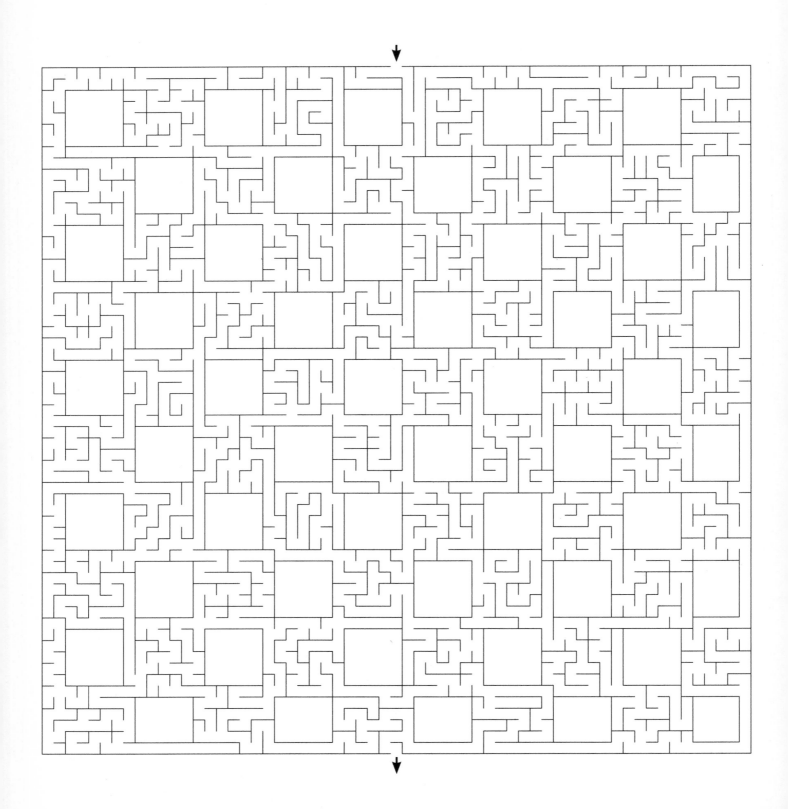

20. BRIDGE MAZE

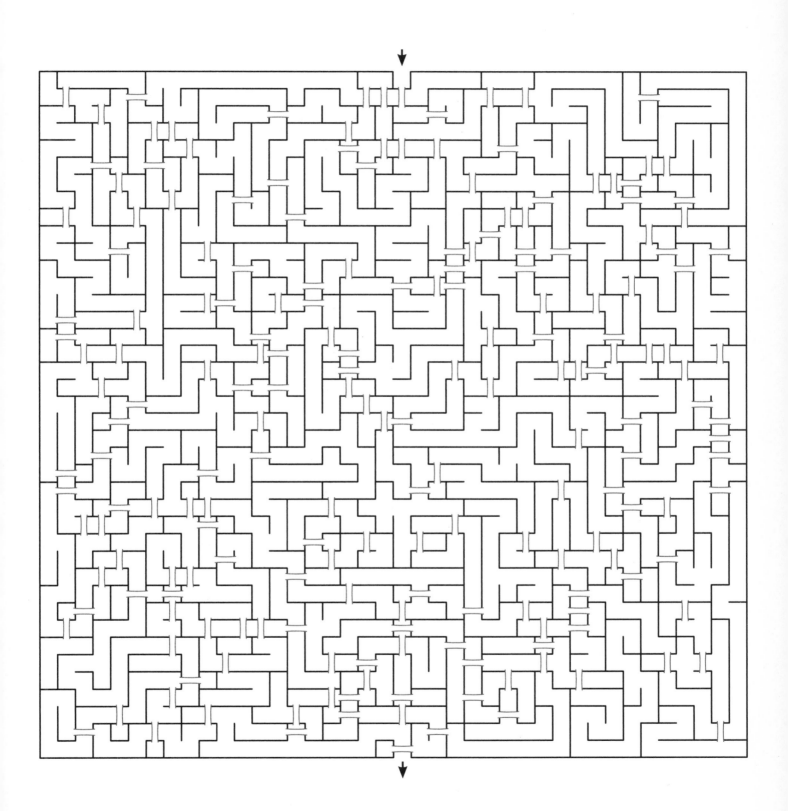

21. VASE MAZE

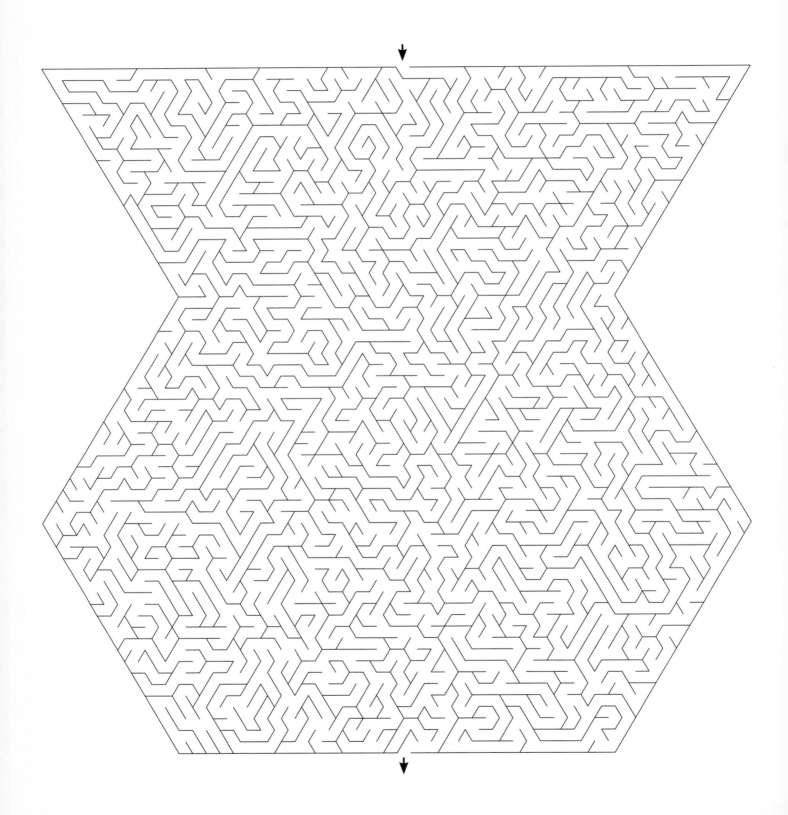

22. MULTI-LEVEL MAZE

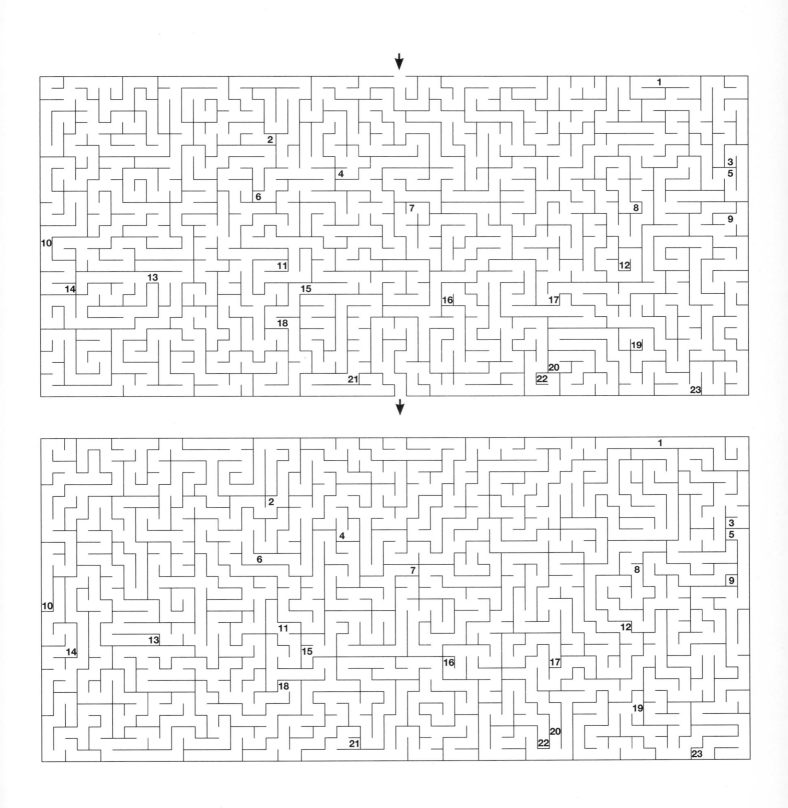

23. CLASSIC MAZE

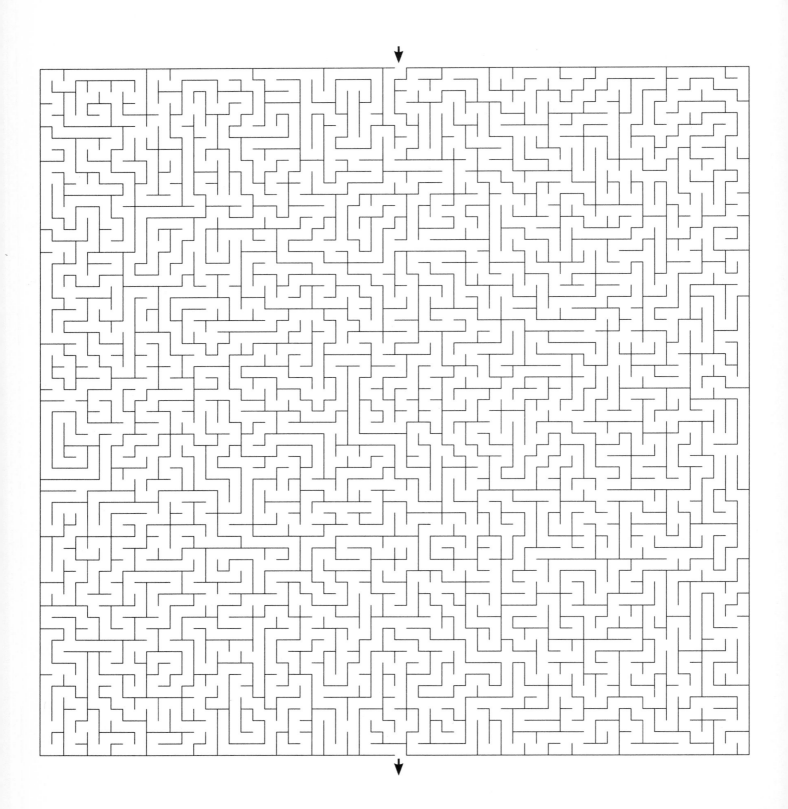

24. CURVING MAZE

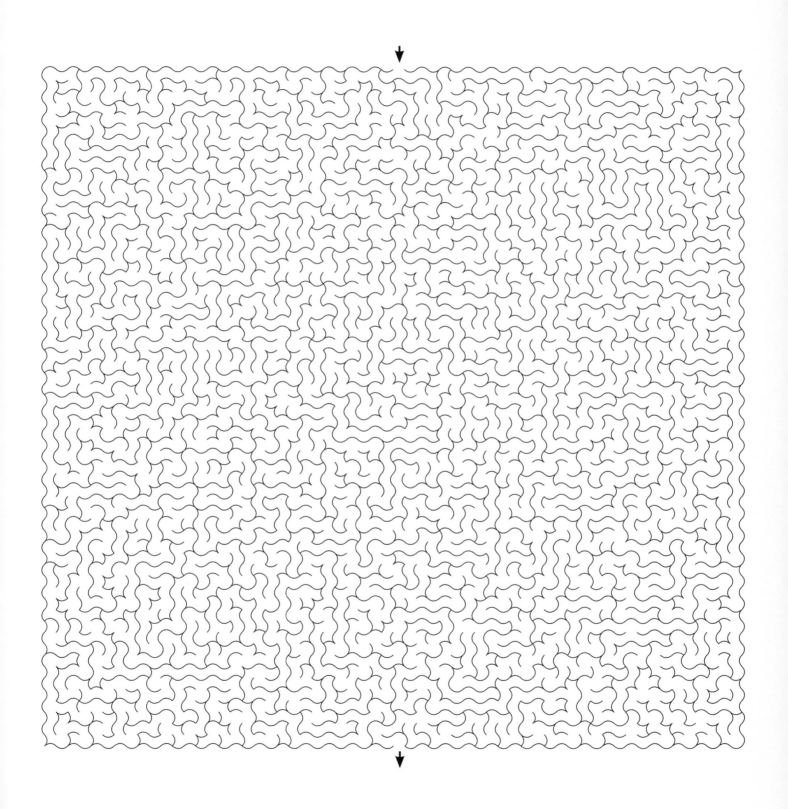

25. WARP MAZE

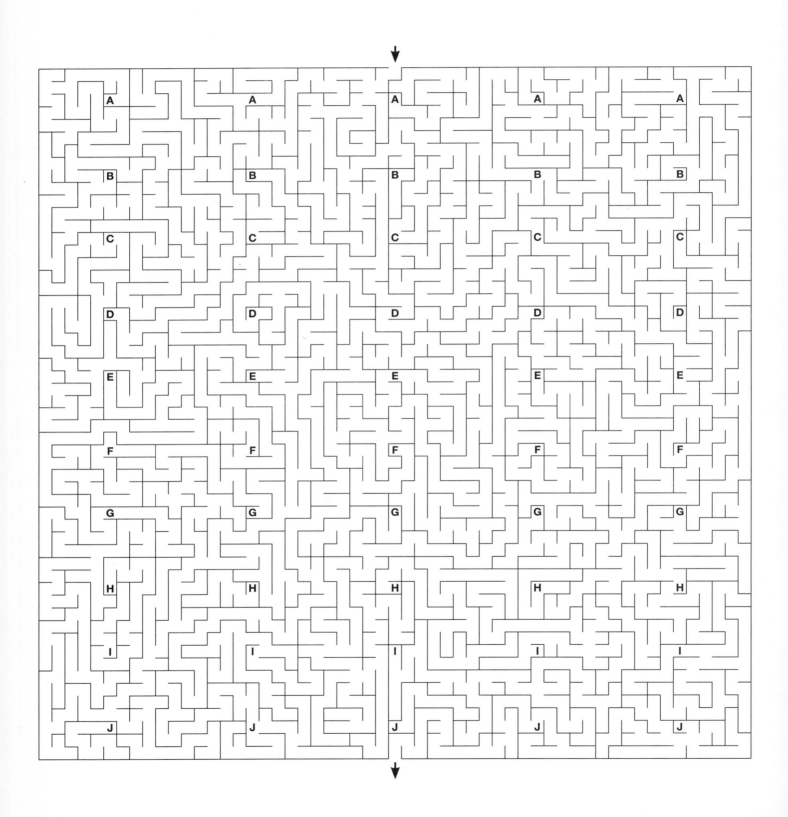

26. BRIDGE MAZE

27. CIRCULAR MAZE

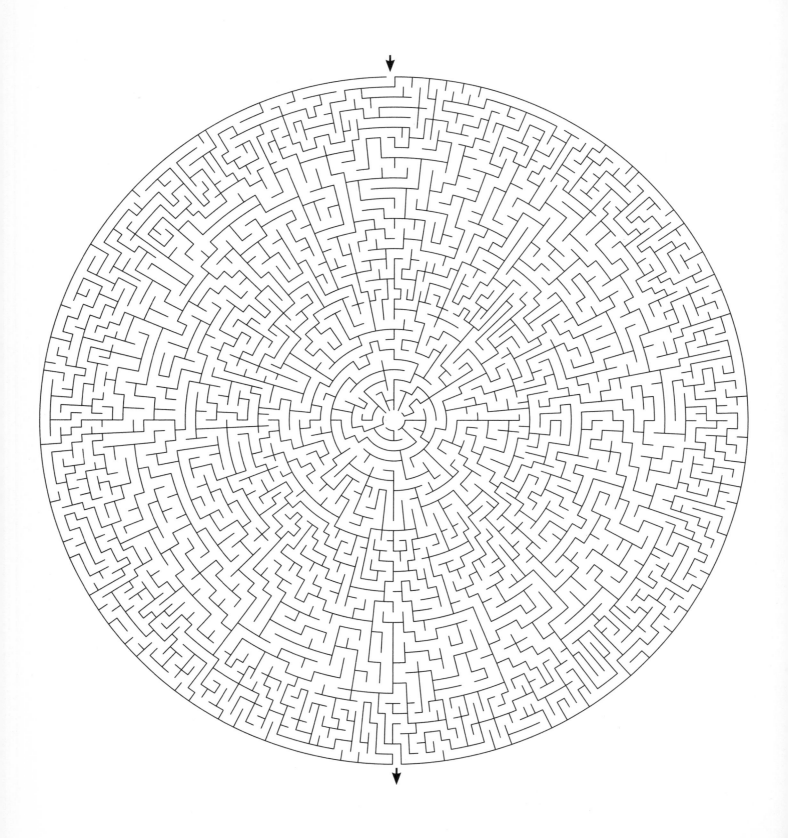

28. TWISTED TRIANGULAR MAZE

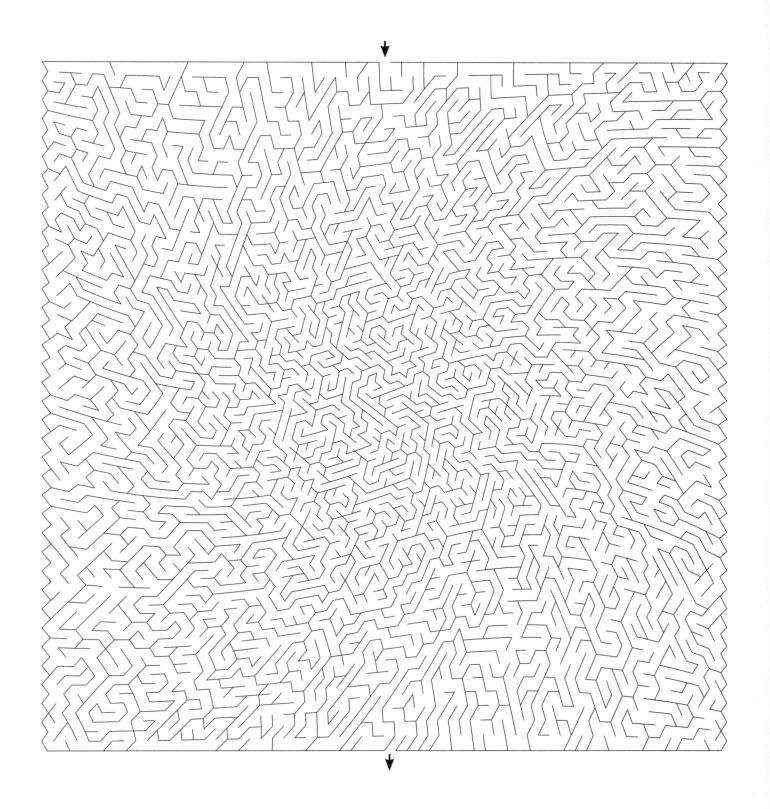

29. HEXAGONAL MAZE

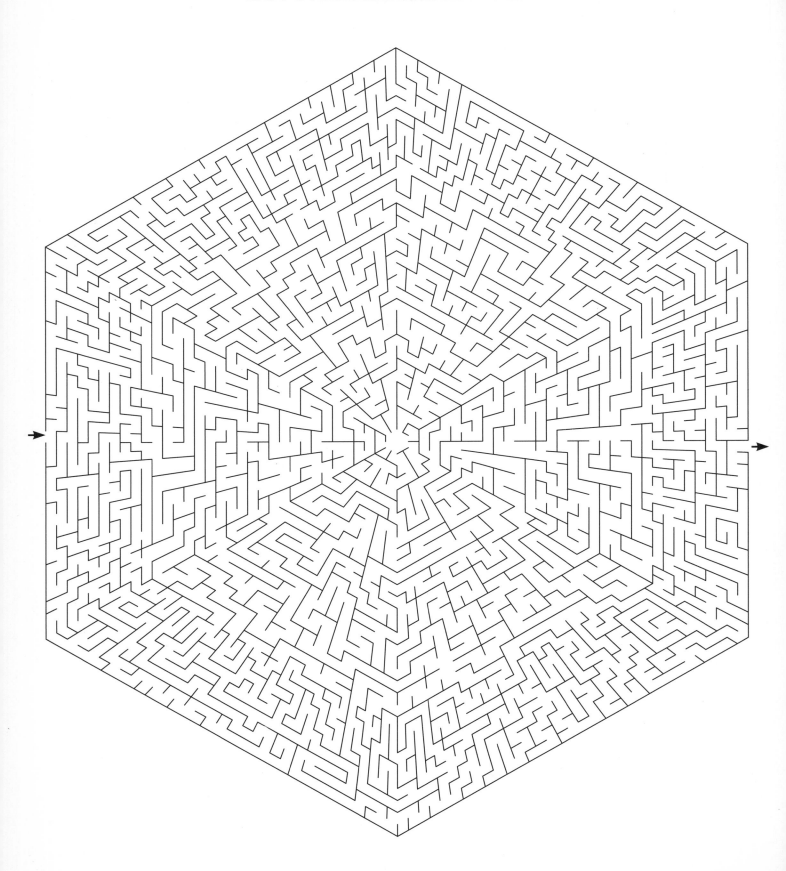

30. HOURGLASS MAZE

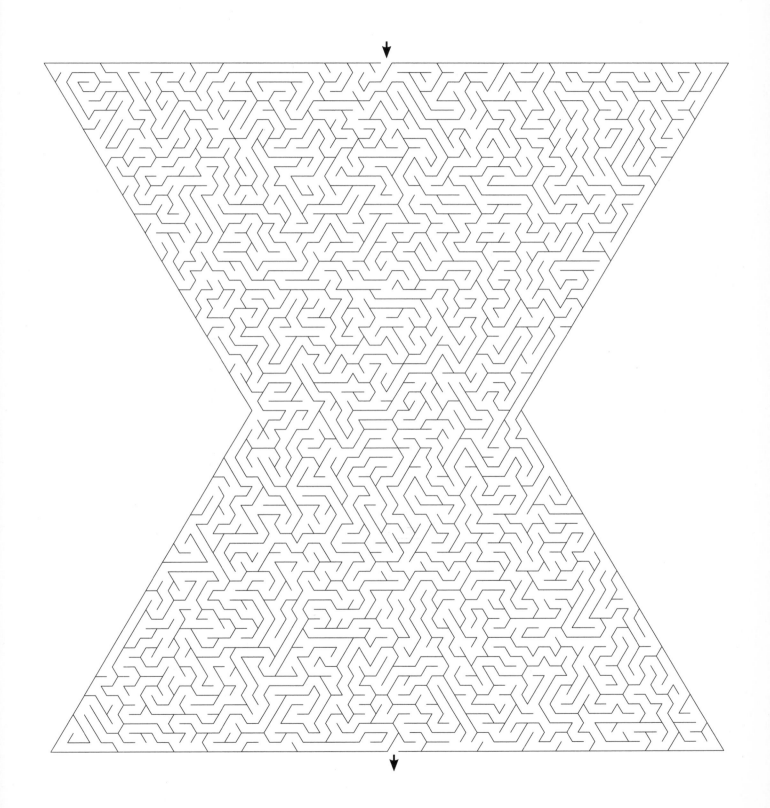

31. CLASSIC MAZE

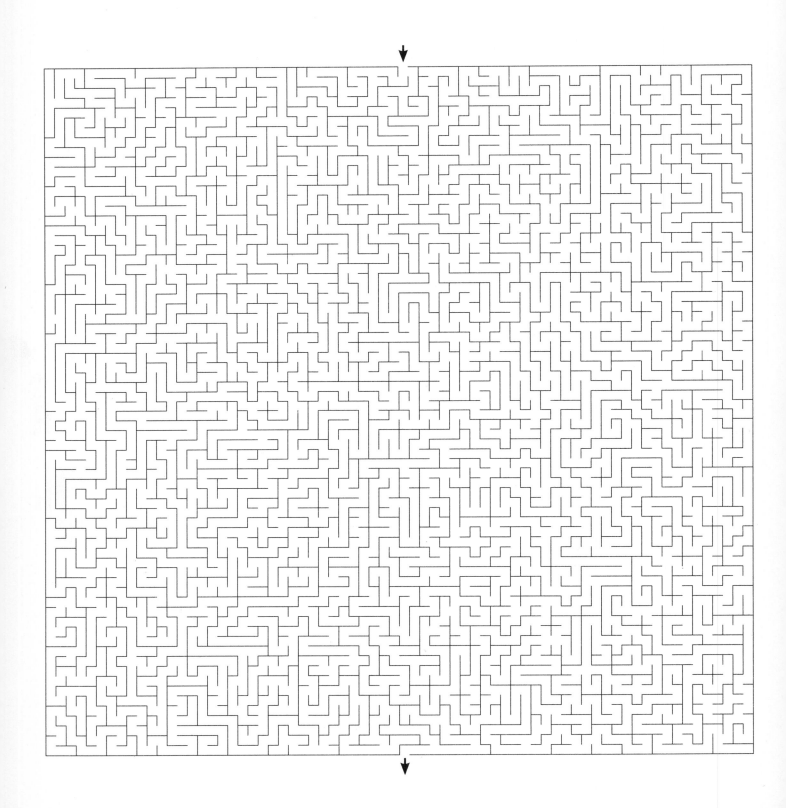

32. DIAMOND MAZE

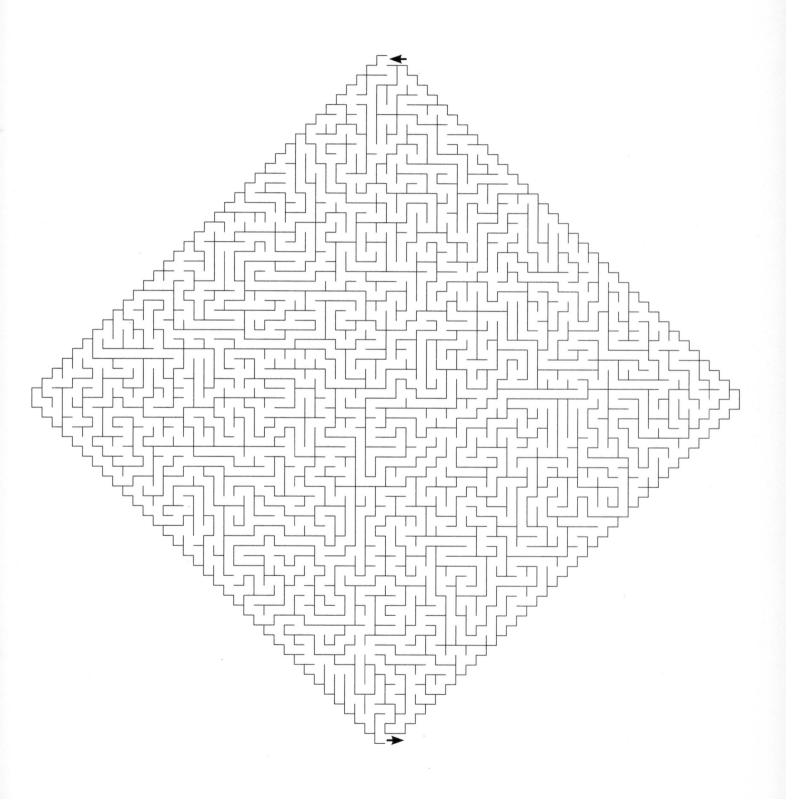

33. ROOMS MAZE

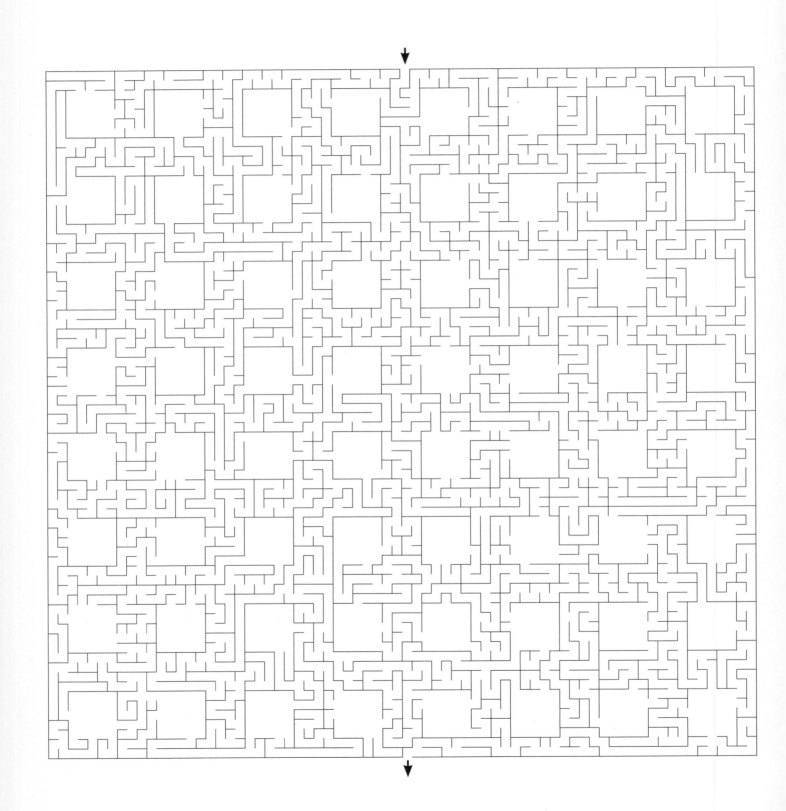

34. INFLATED BRIDGE MAZE

35. OCTAGONAL MAZE

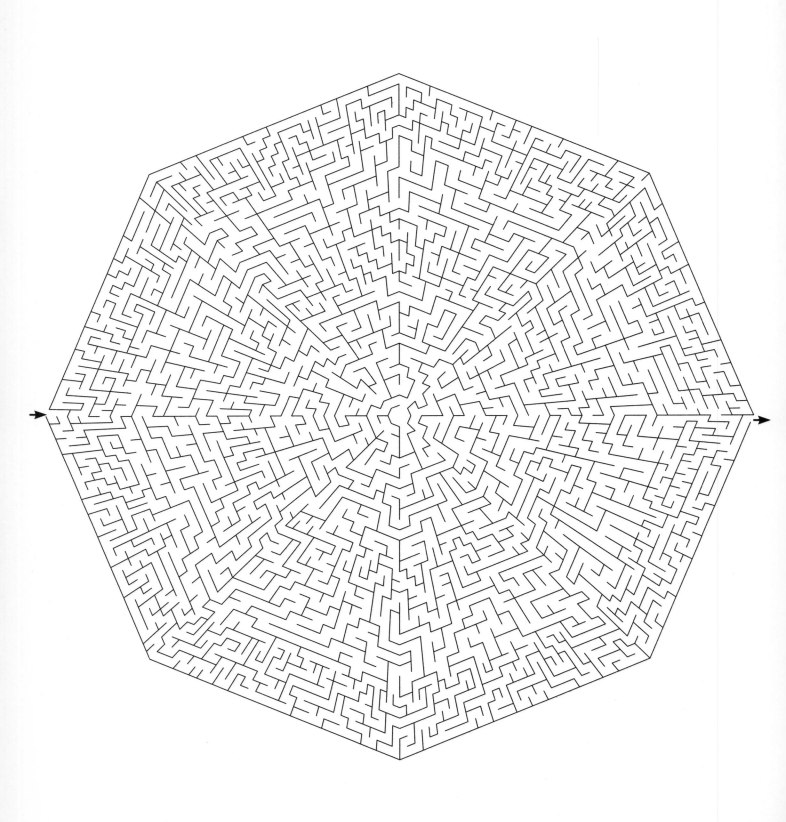

36. TRIANGULAR MAZE

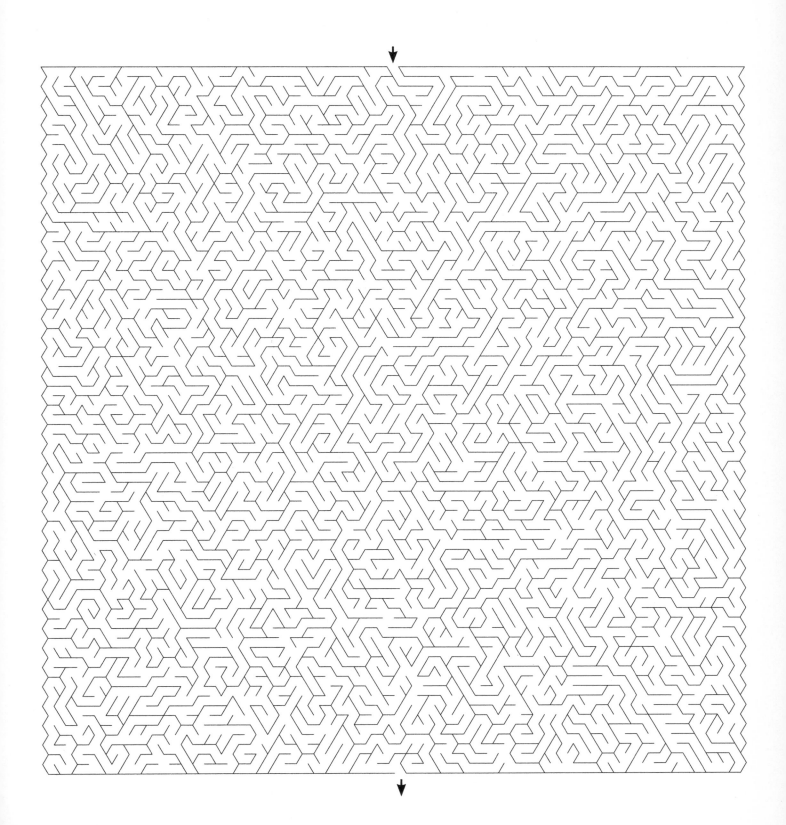

37. X-SHAPED MAZE

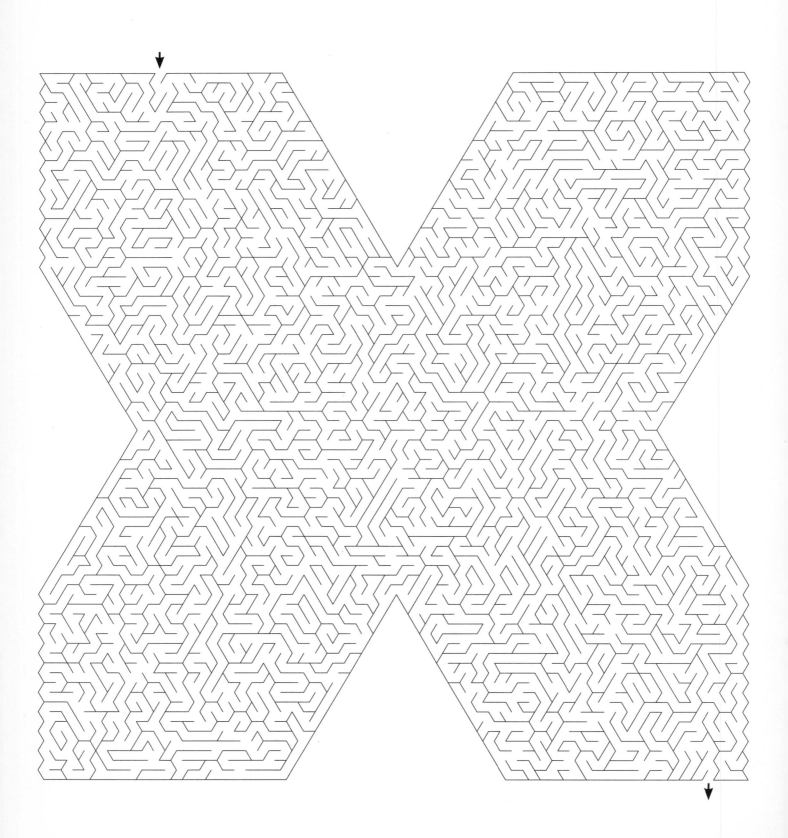

38. MULTI-LEVEL MAZE

39. CIRCULAR MAZE

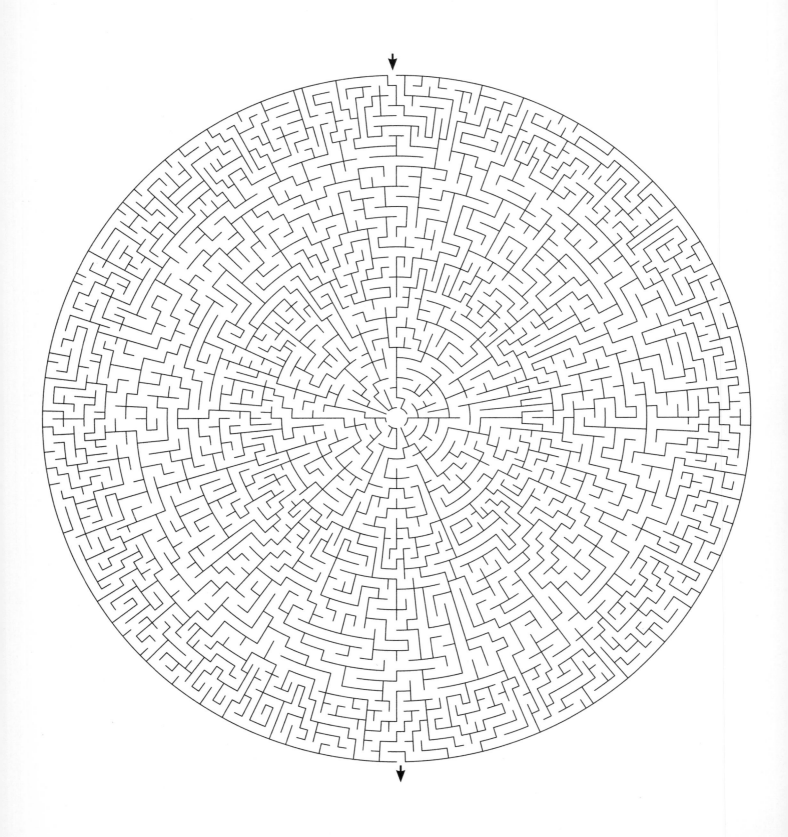

40. CORRIDORS MAZE

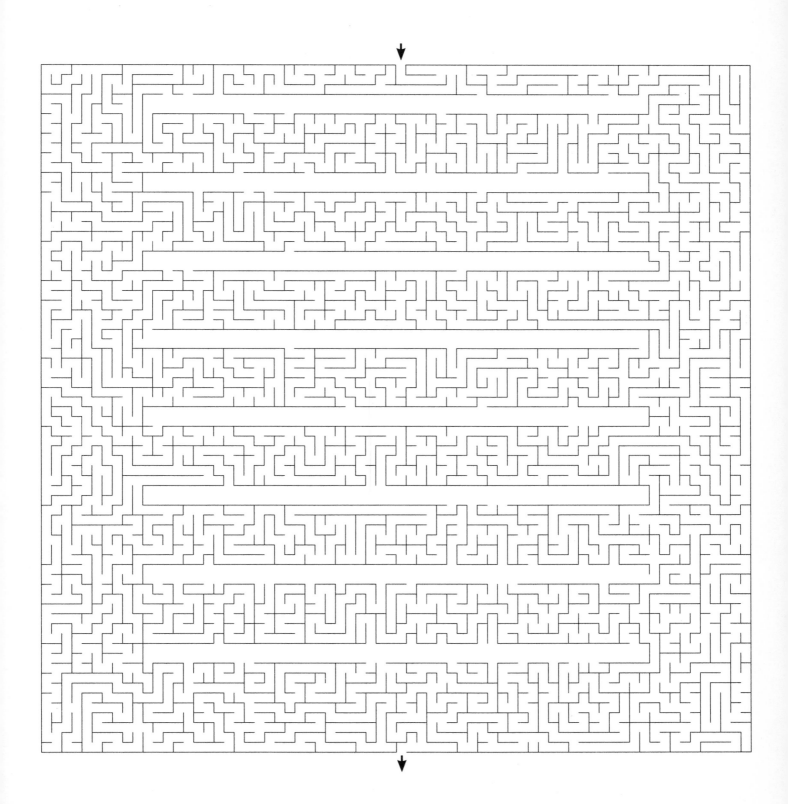

41. CURVING MAZE

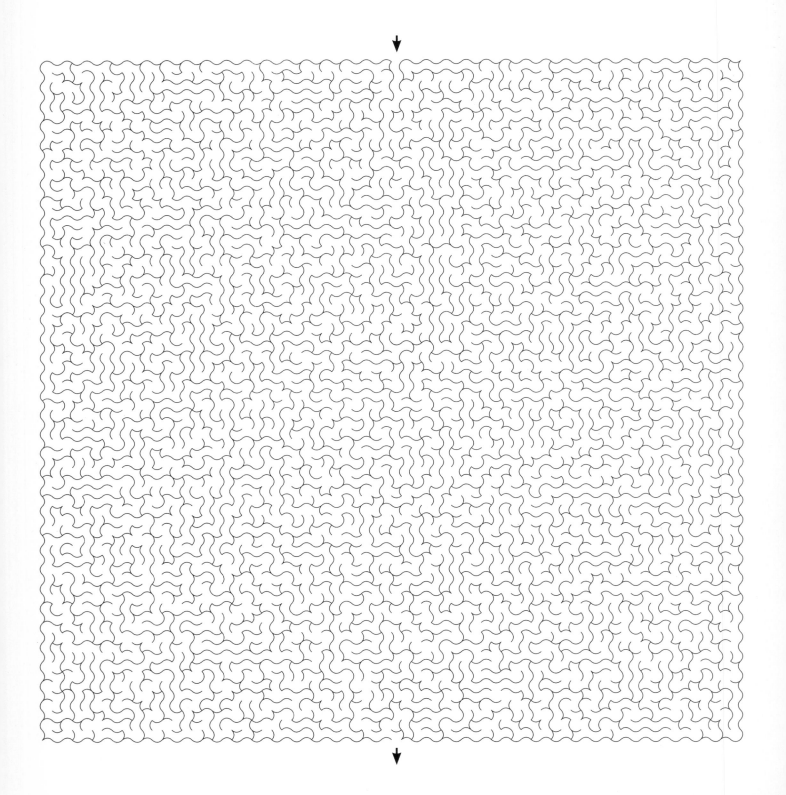

42. GAP MAZE

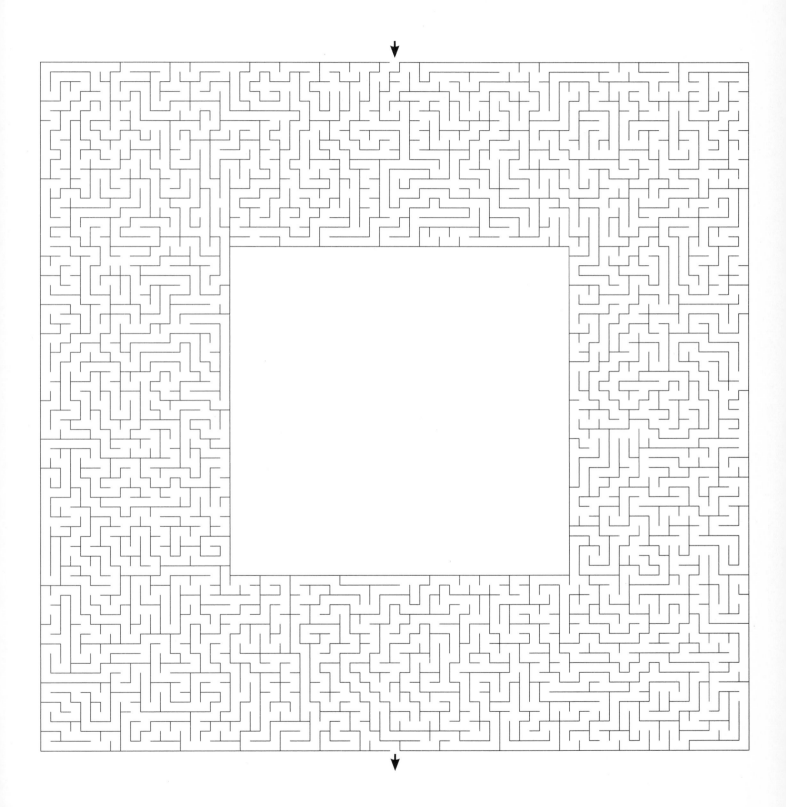

43. TWISTED MAZE

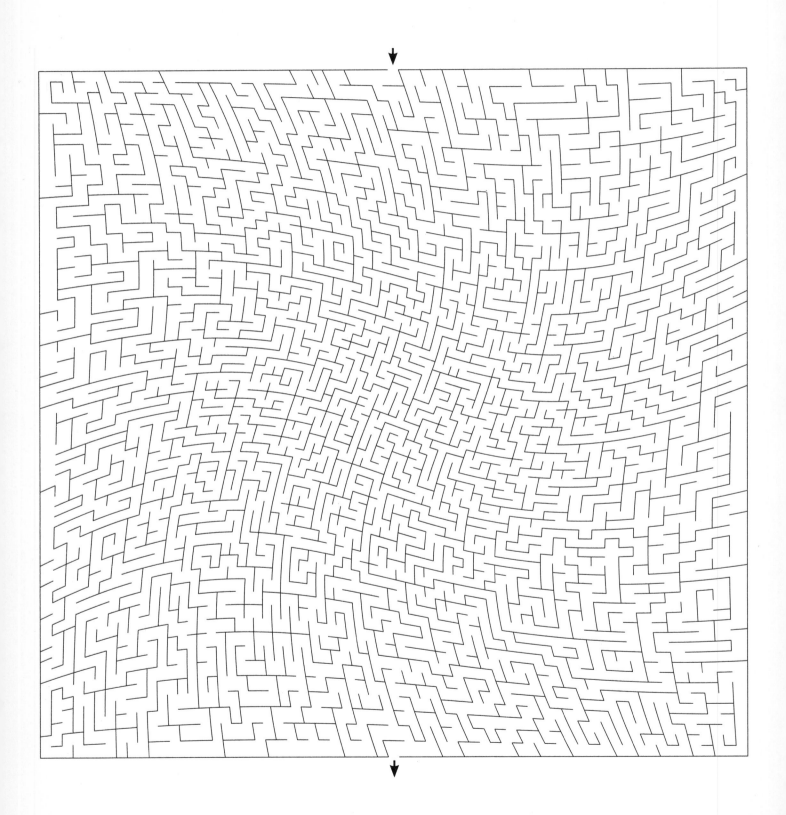

44. PENTAGONAL MAZE

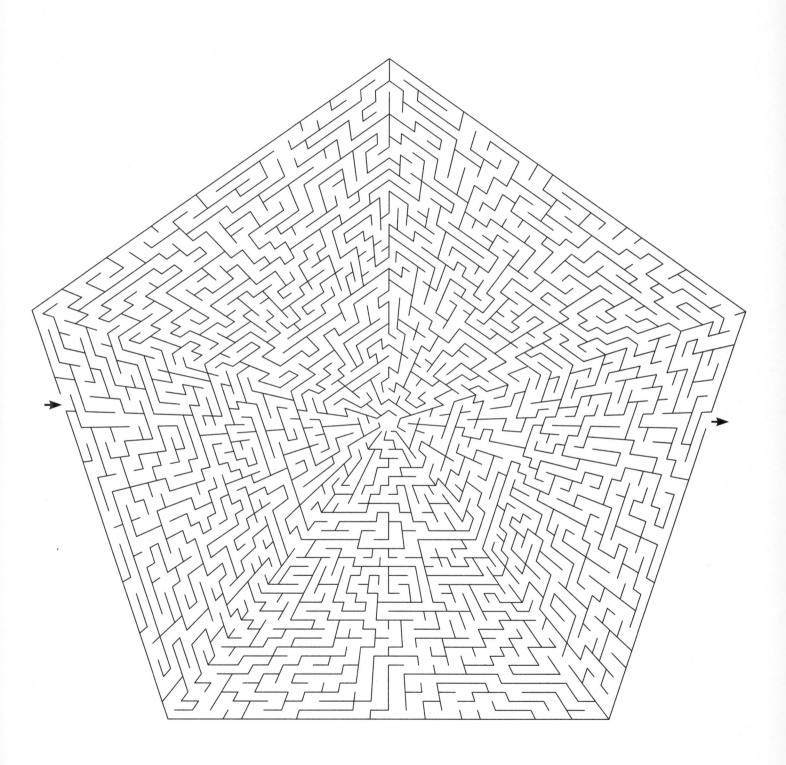

45. WARP MAZE

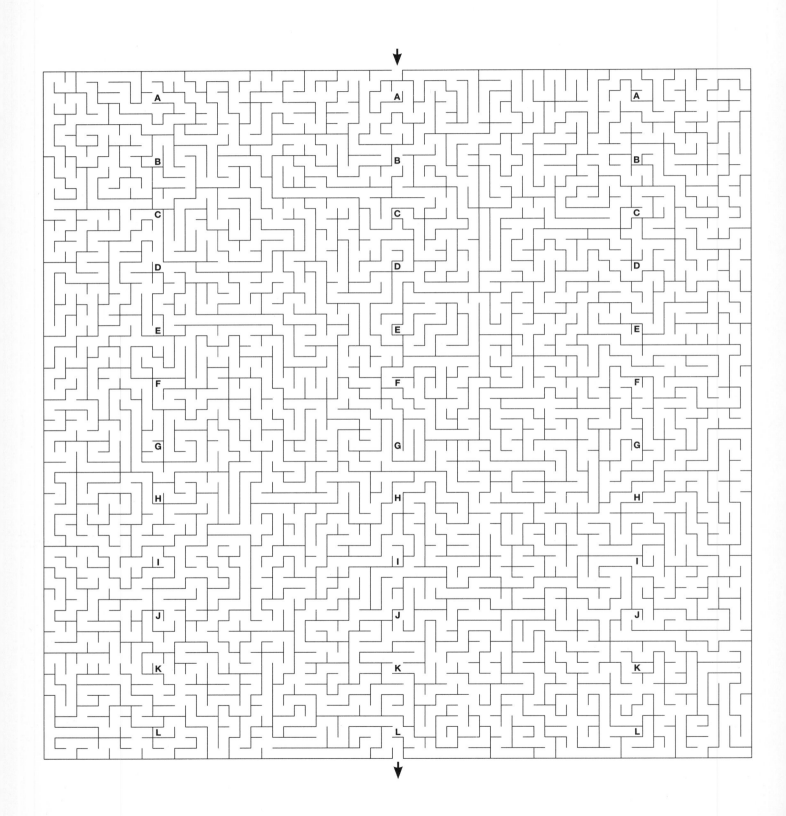

46. CURVING MAZE

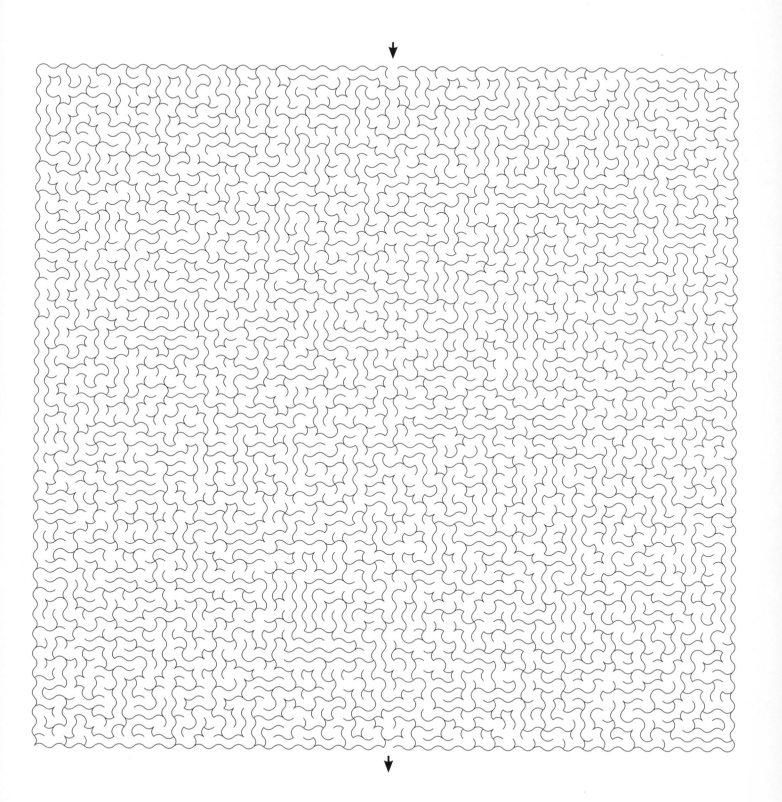

47. BRIDGE MAZE

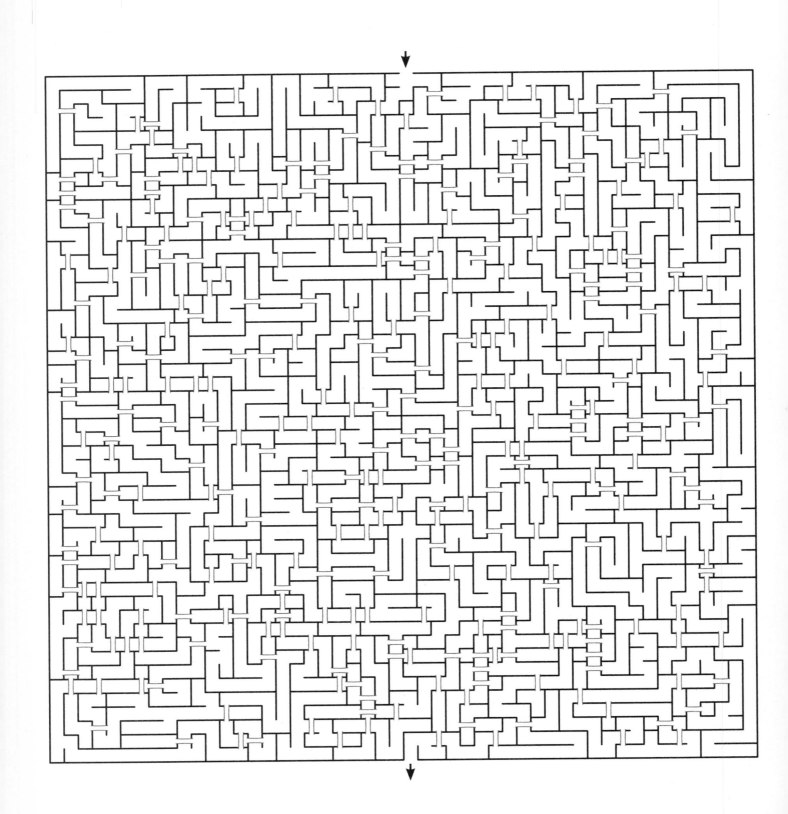

48. ROOM MAZE

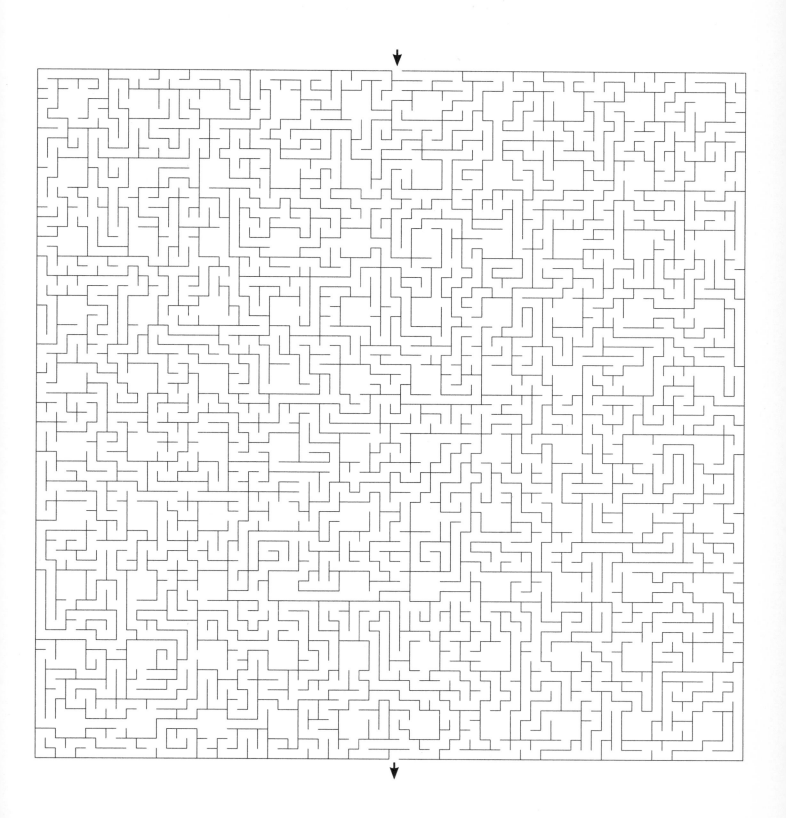

49. CIRCULAR MAZE

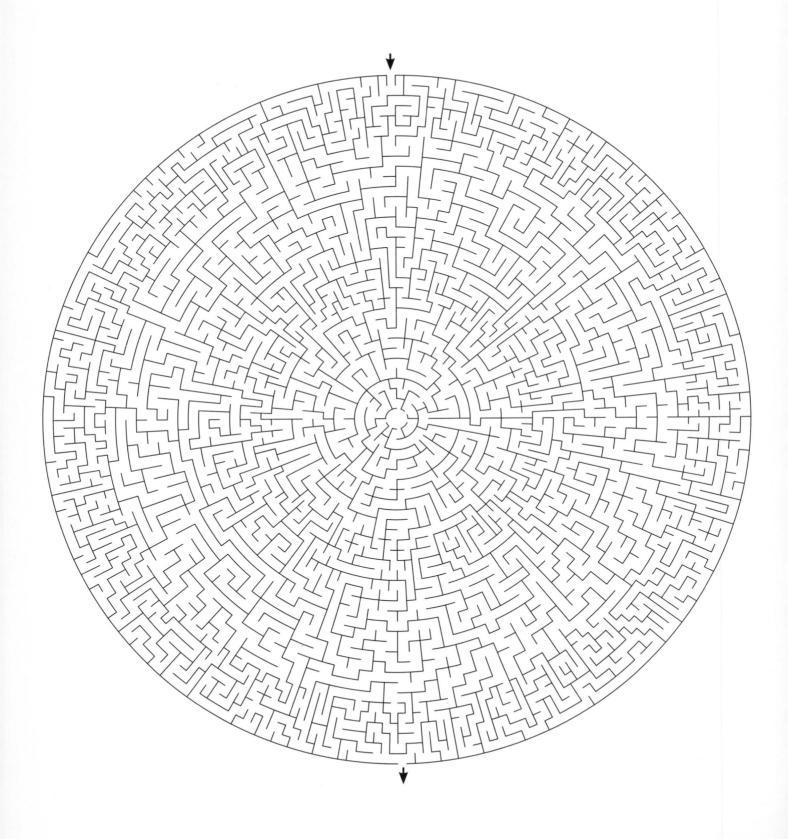

50. CLASSIC MAZE

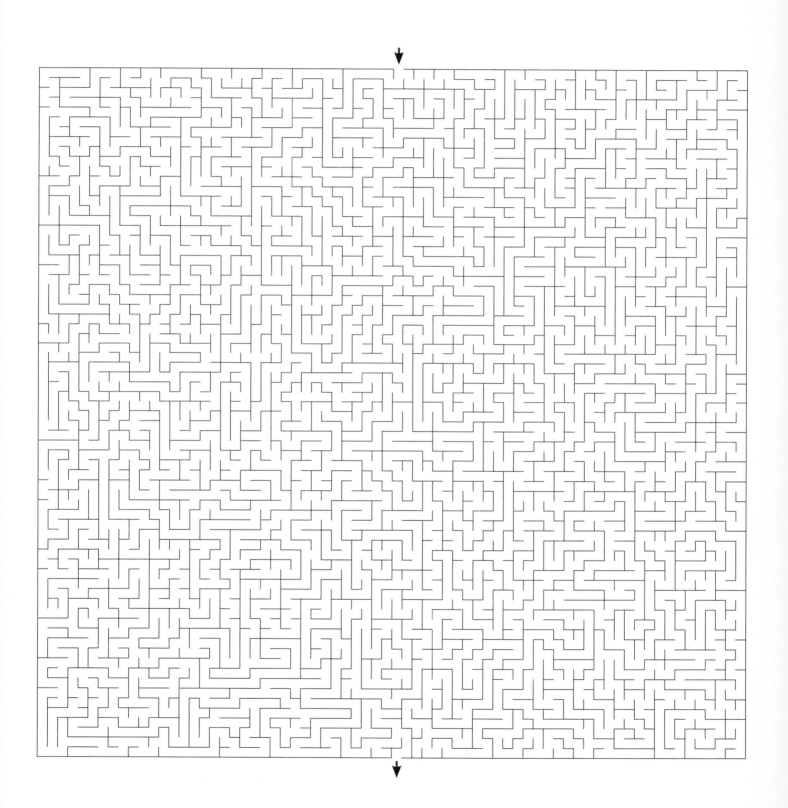

51. BRIDGE MAZE

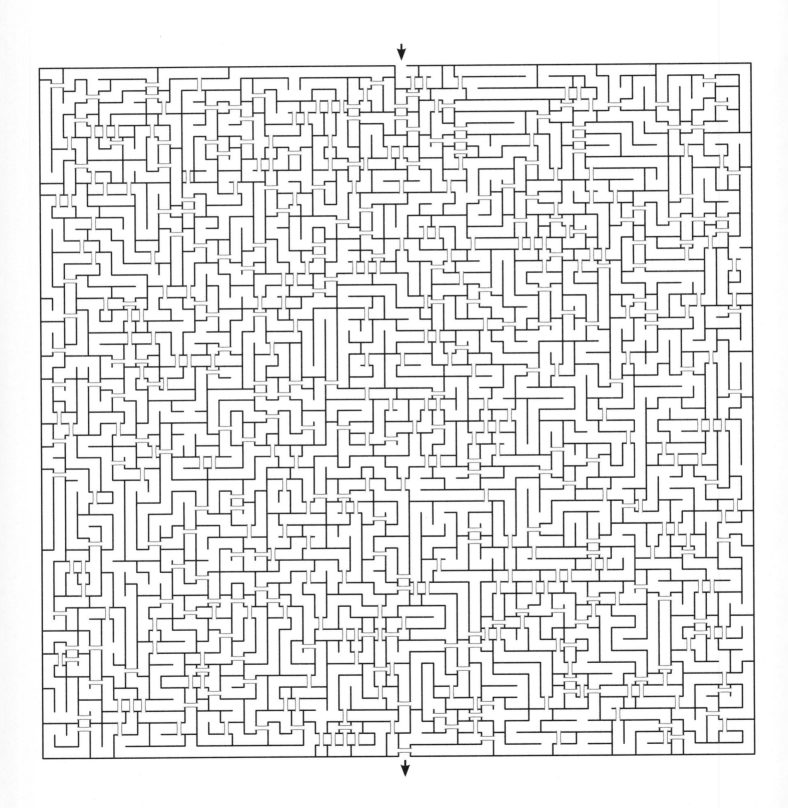

52. HOURGLASS MAZE

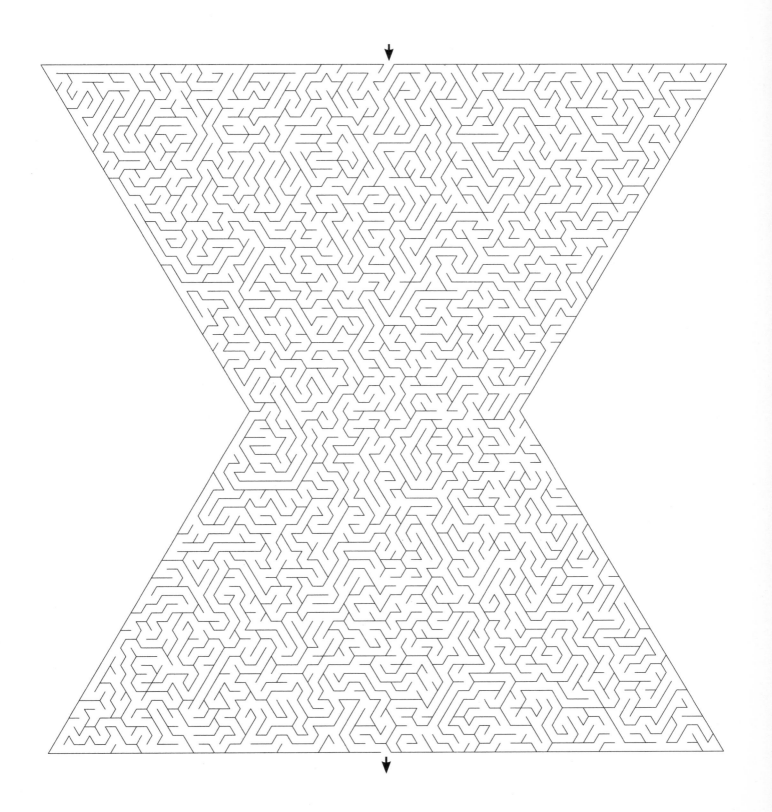

53. HEXAGONAL MAZE

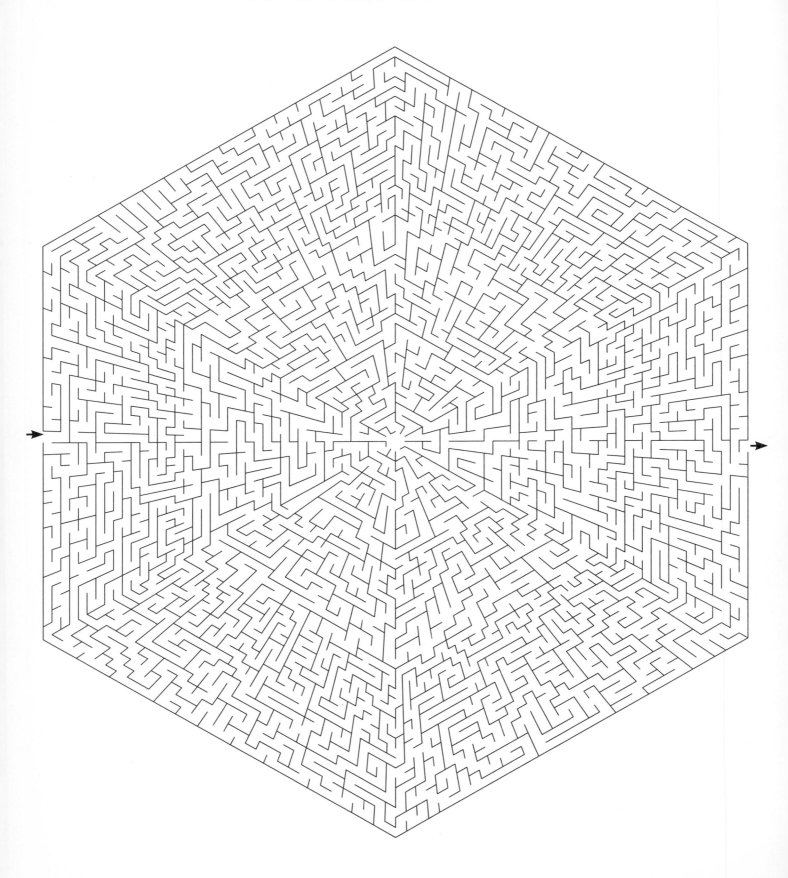

54. CLASSIC MAZE

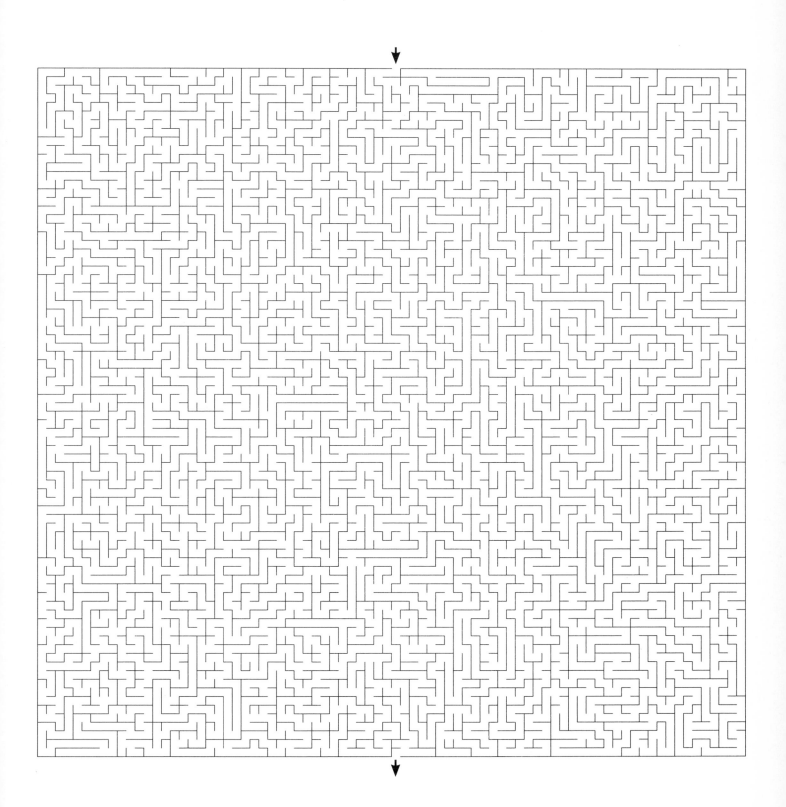

55. TRIANGULAR MAZE

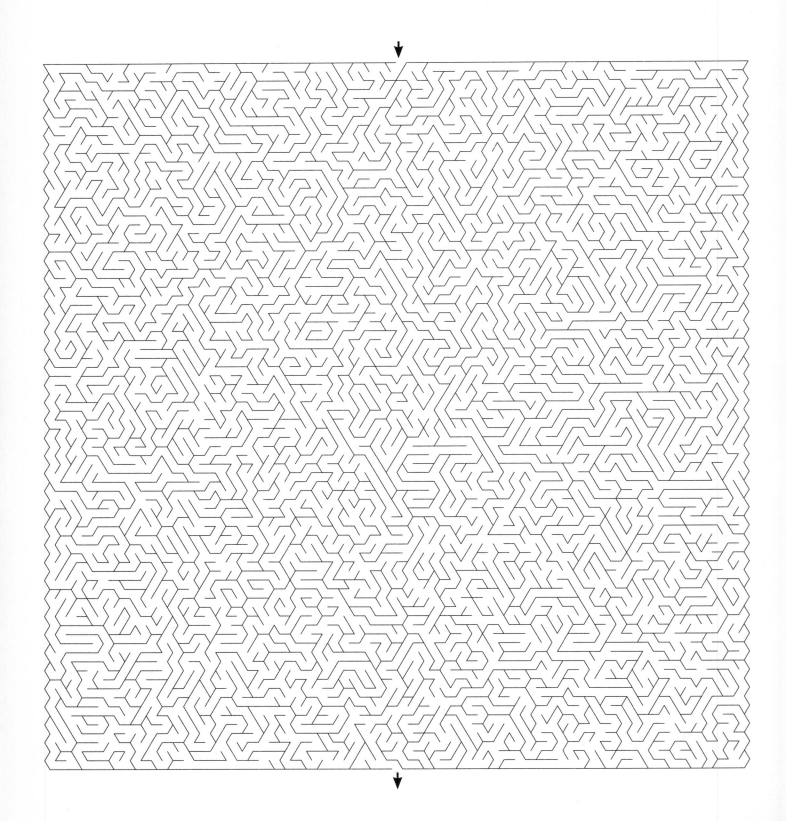

56. ROOMS MAZE

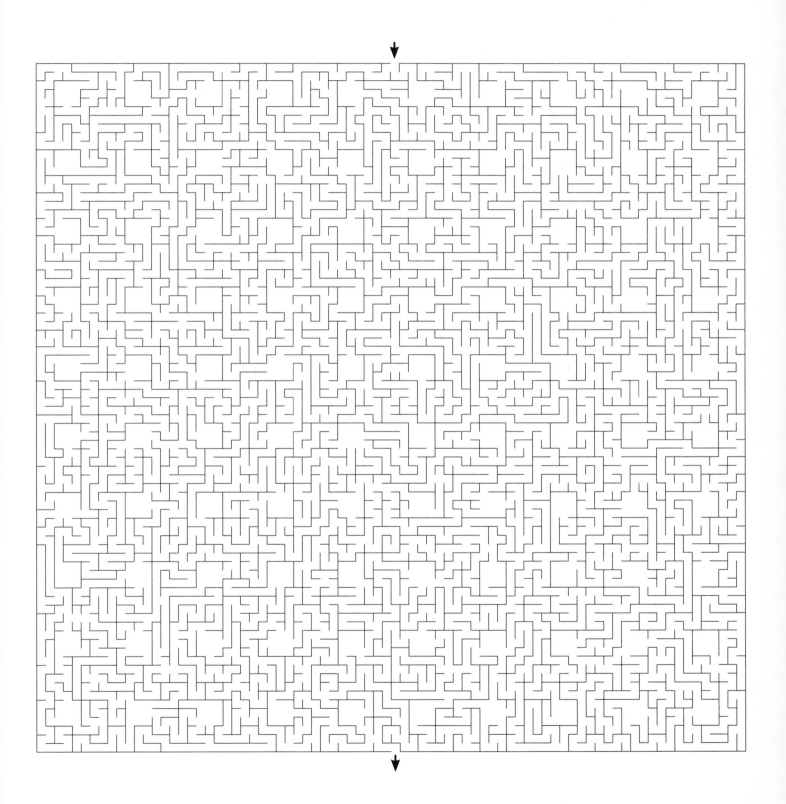

57. INFLATED MAZE

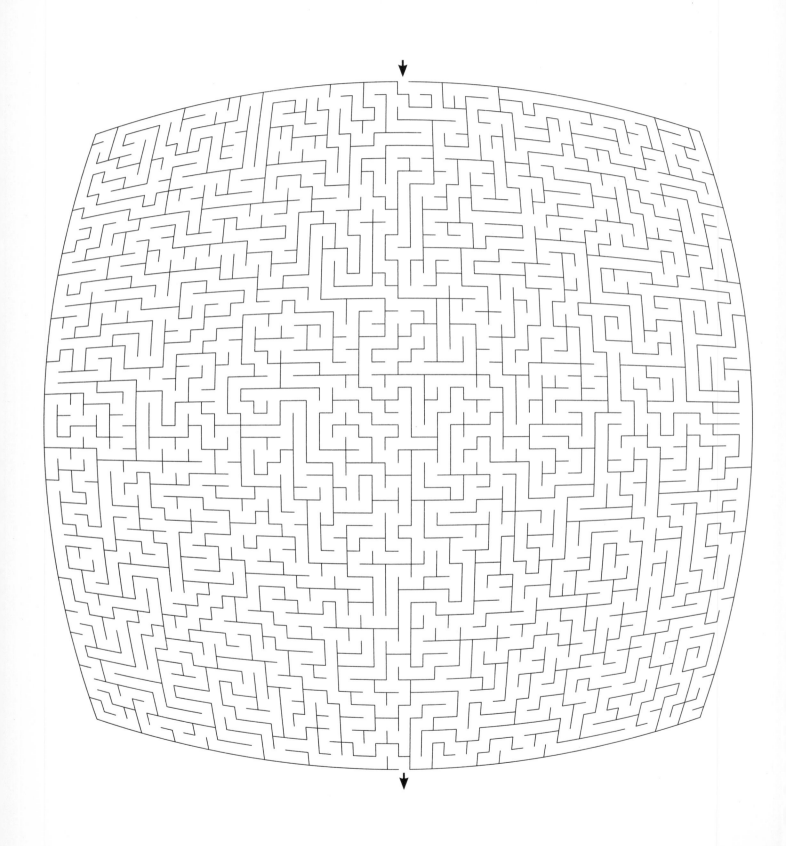

58. CORRIDORS MAZE

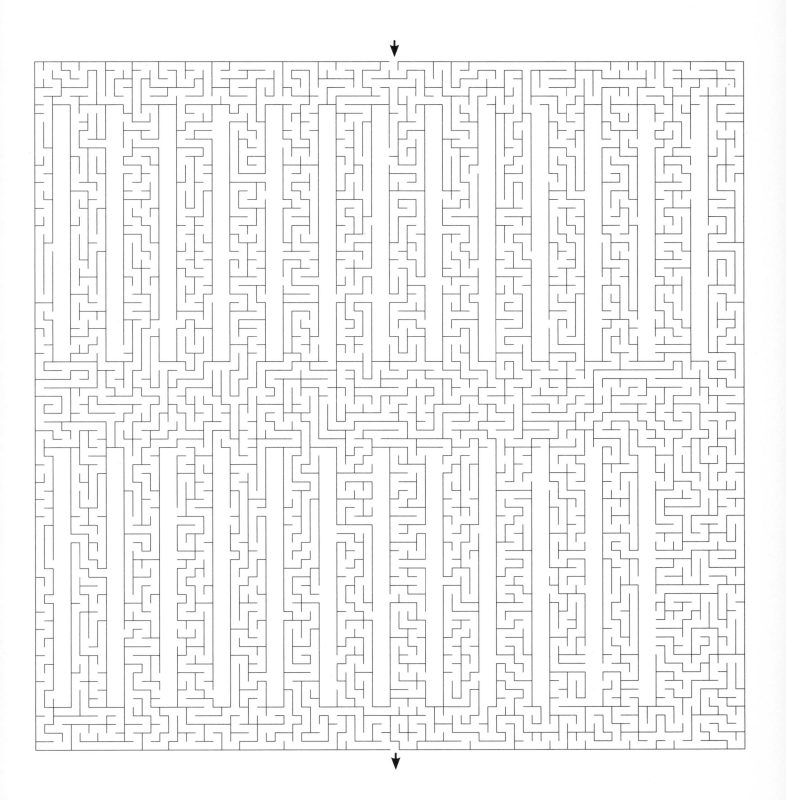

59. WARP MAZE

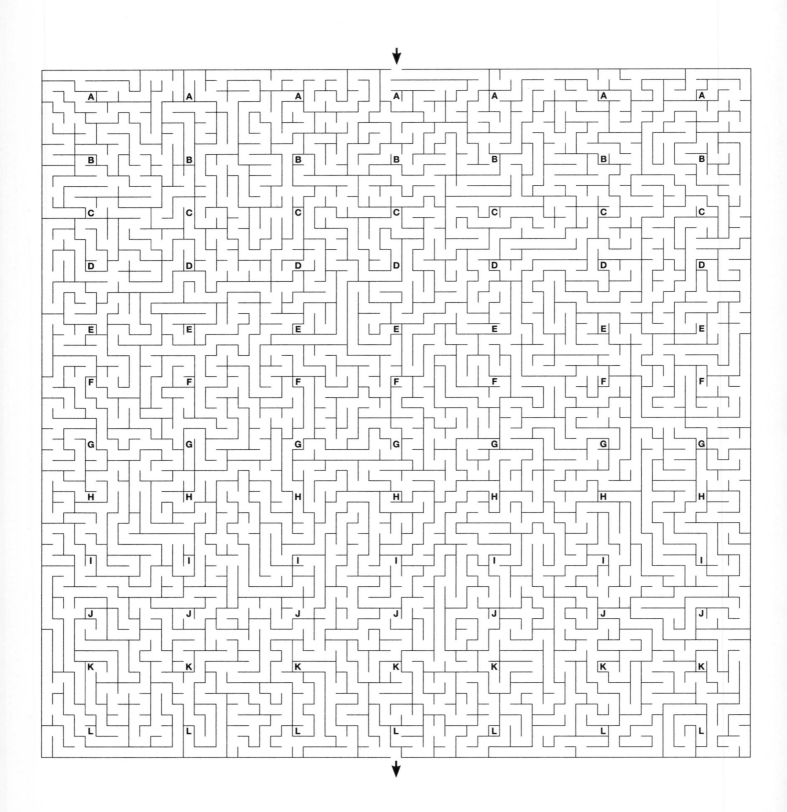

60. PENTAGONAL MAZE

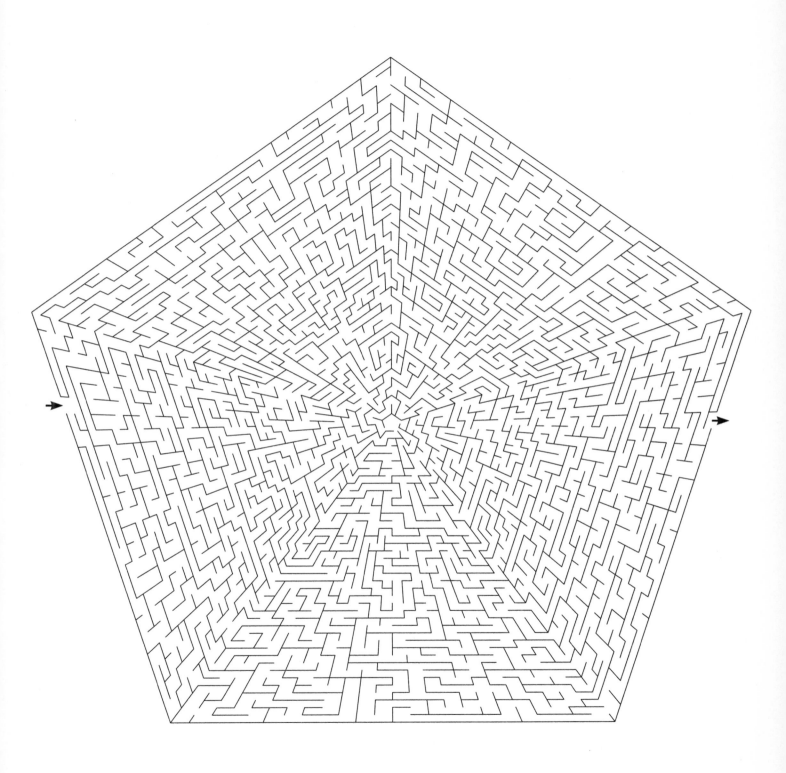

61. CURVING MAZE

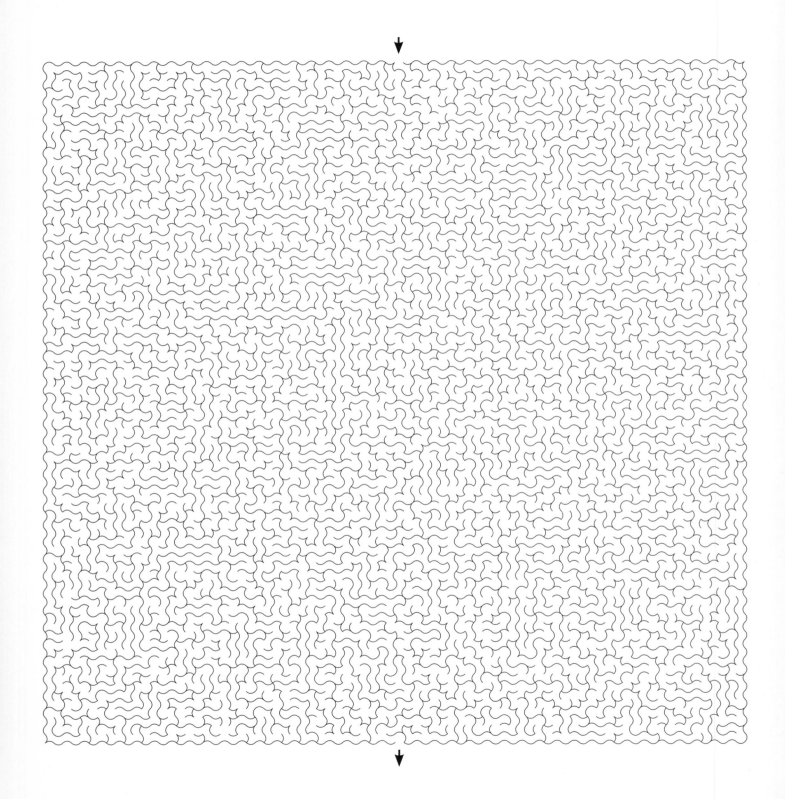

62. GAP MAZE

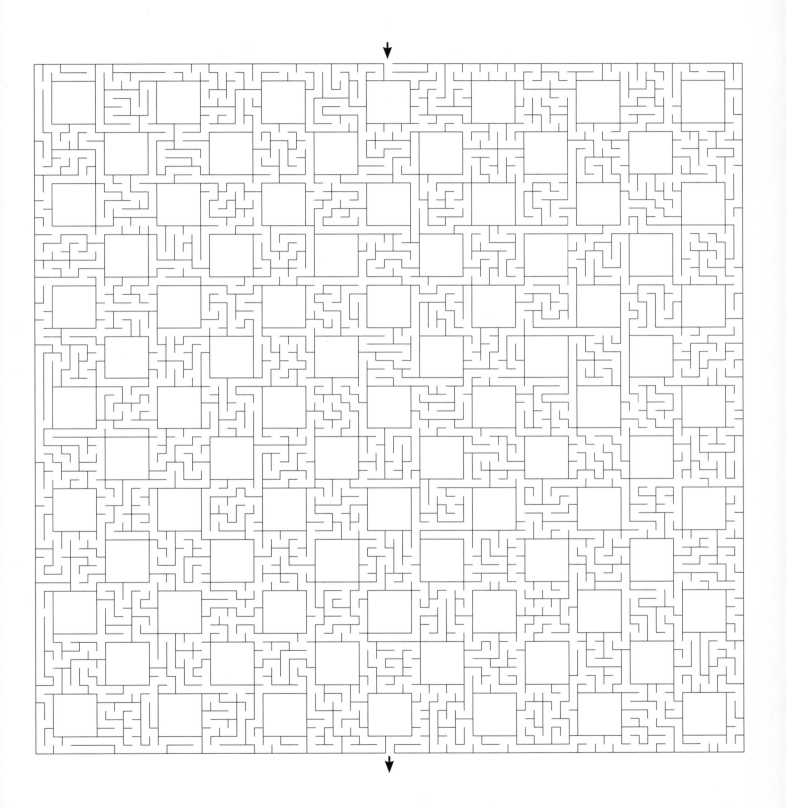

63. MULTI-LEVEL MAZE

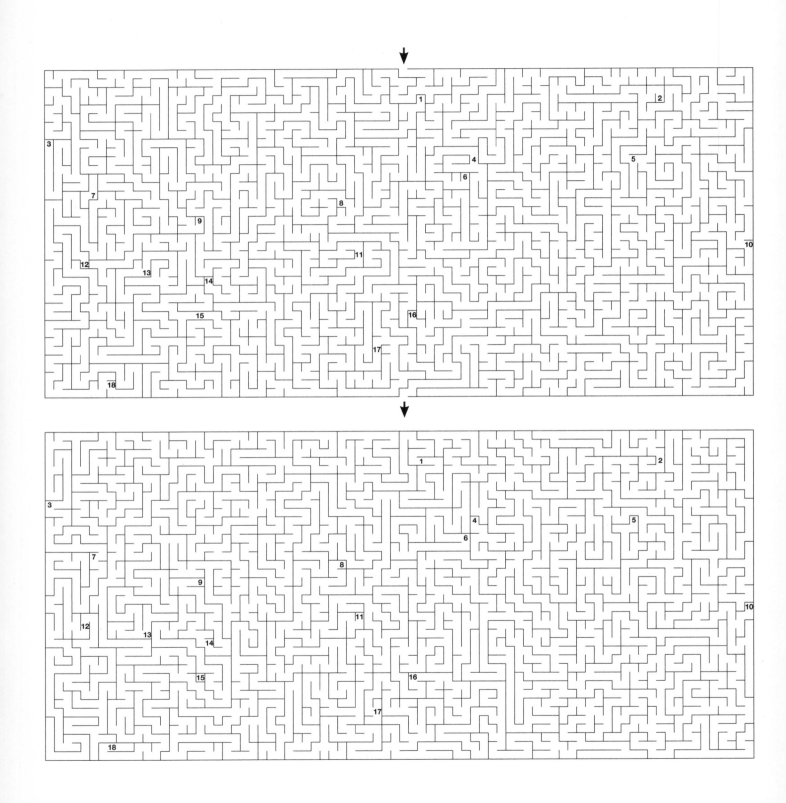

64. CIRCULAR MAZE

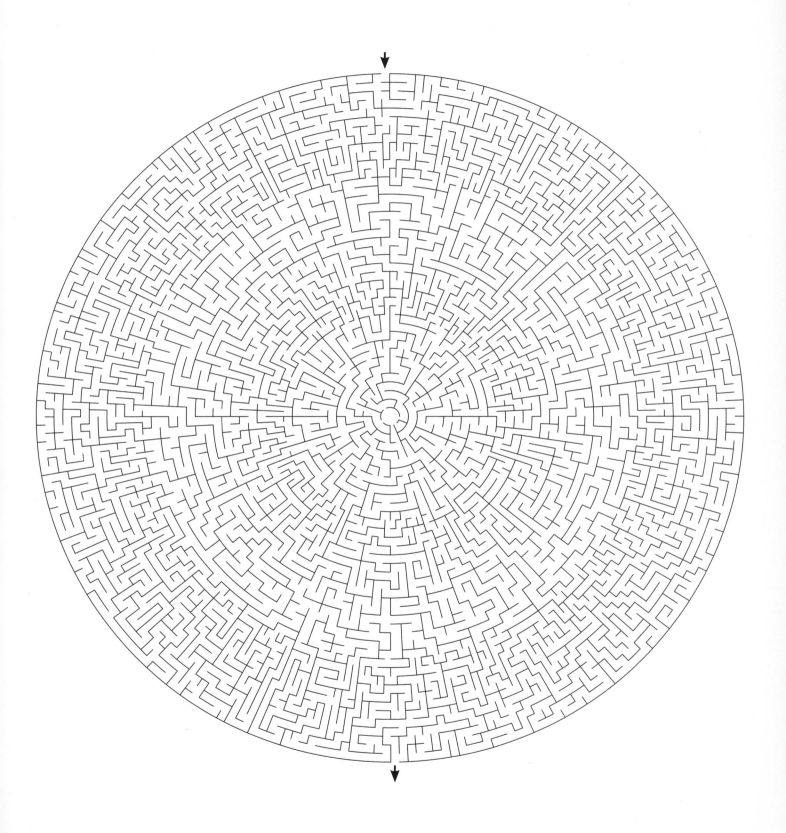

65. HEXAGONAL MAZE

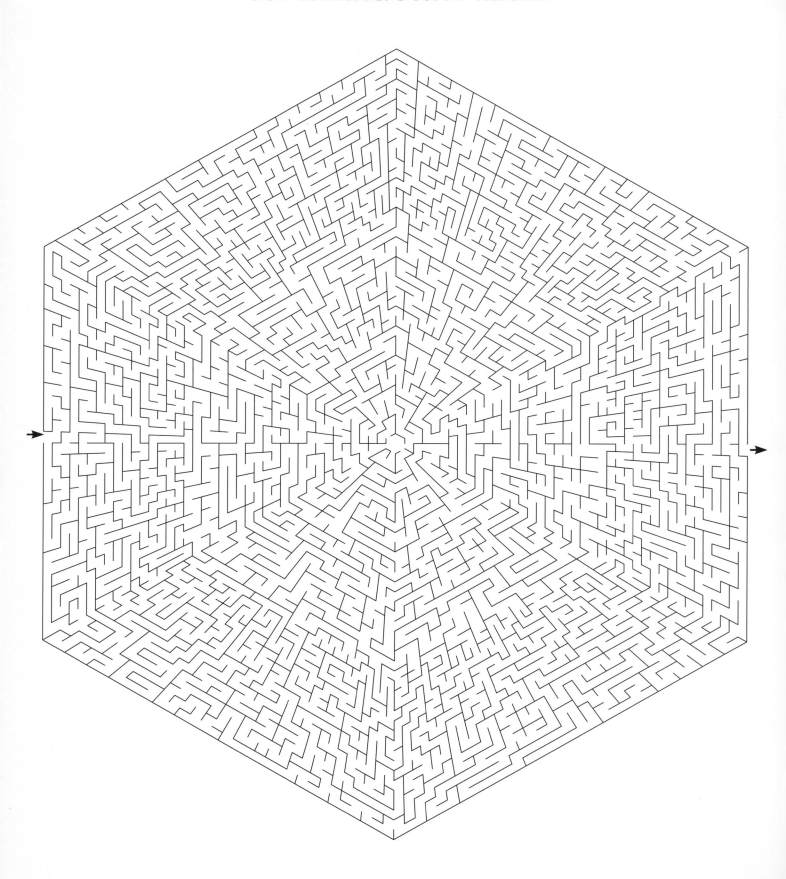

66. CLASSIC MAZE

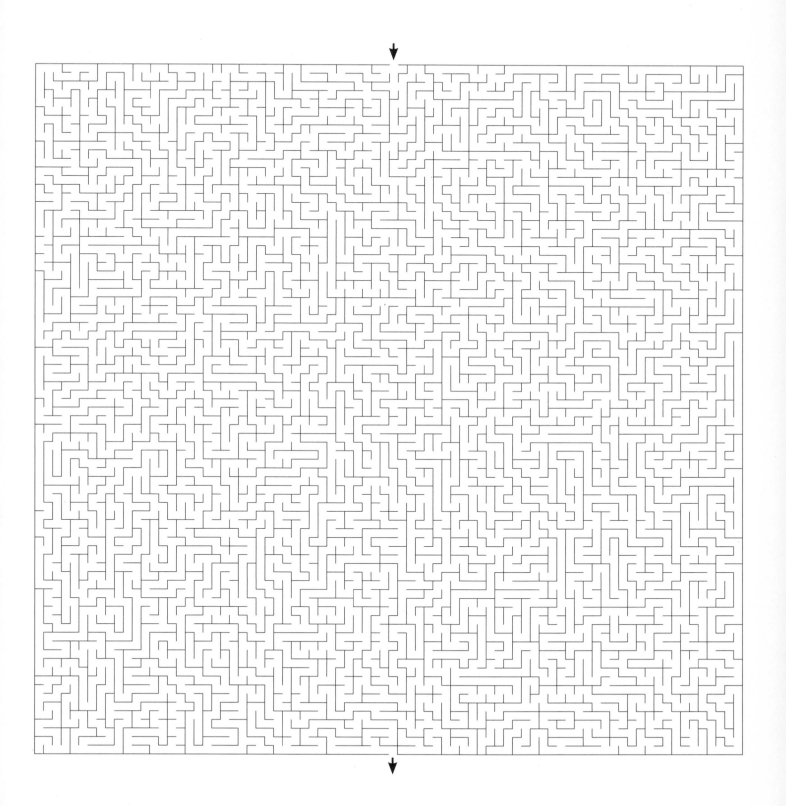

67. TWISTED TRIANGULAR MAZE

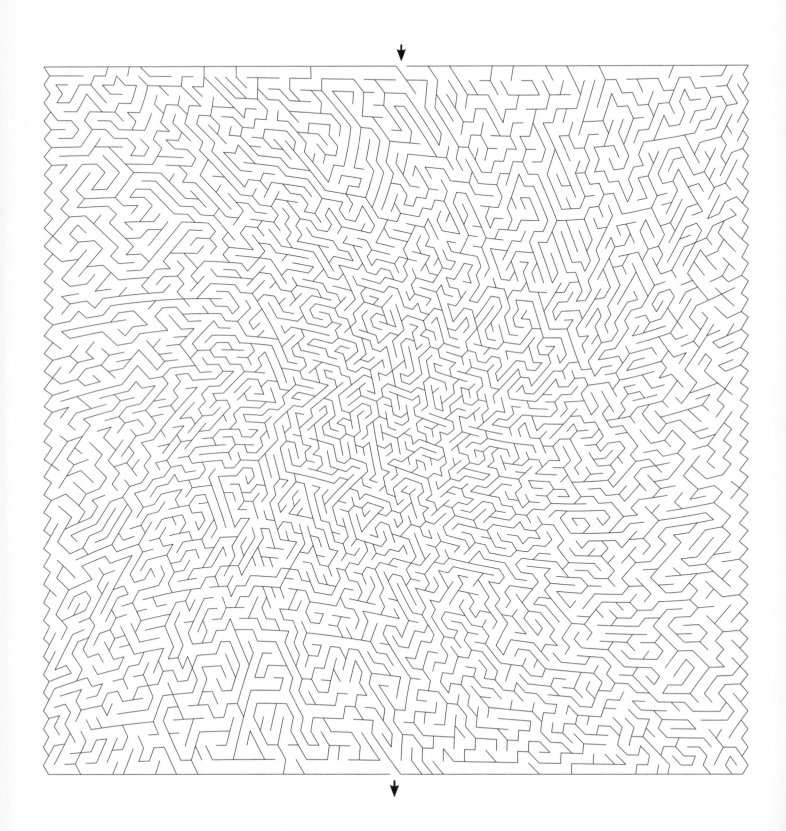

68. BRIDGE MAZE

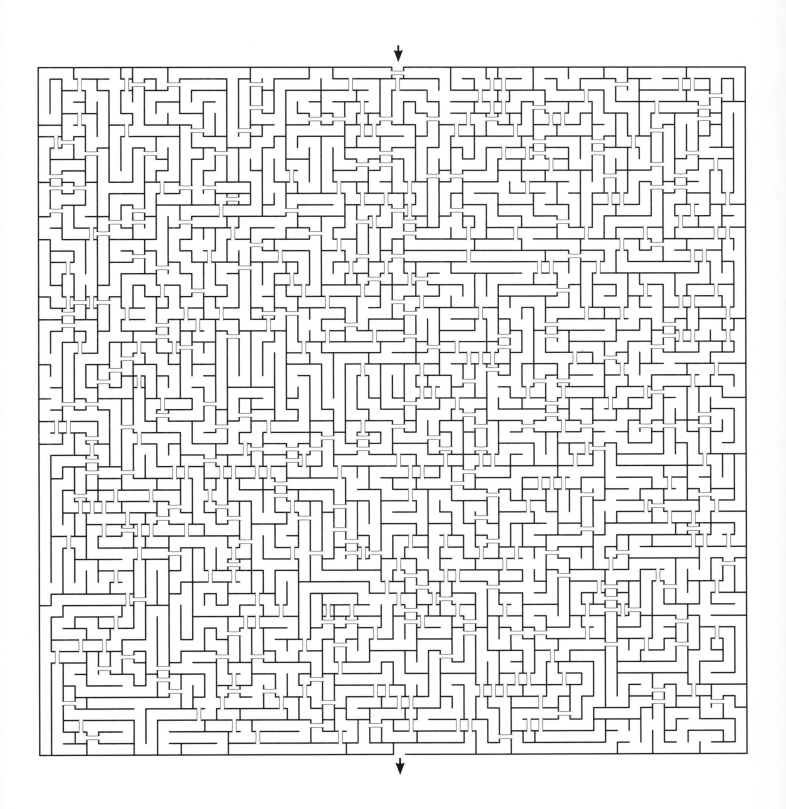

69. CIRCULAR MAZE

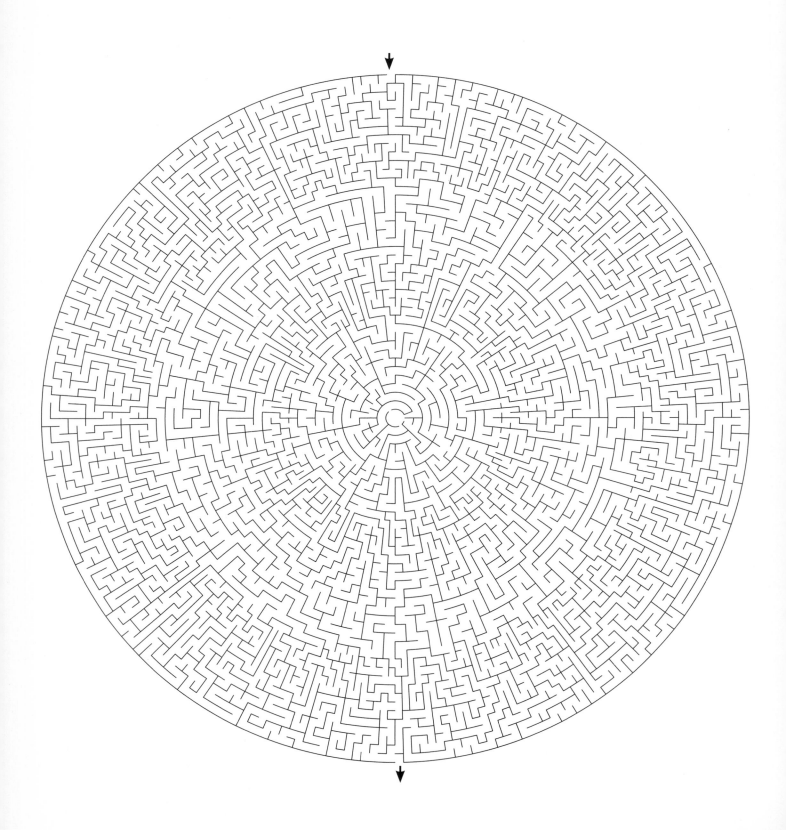

70. ZIGZAG MAZE

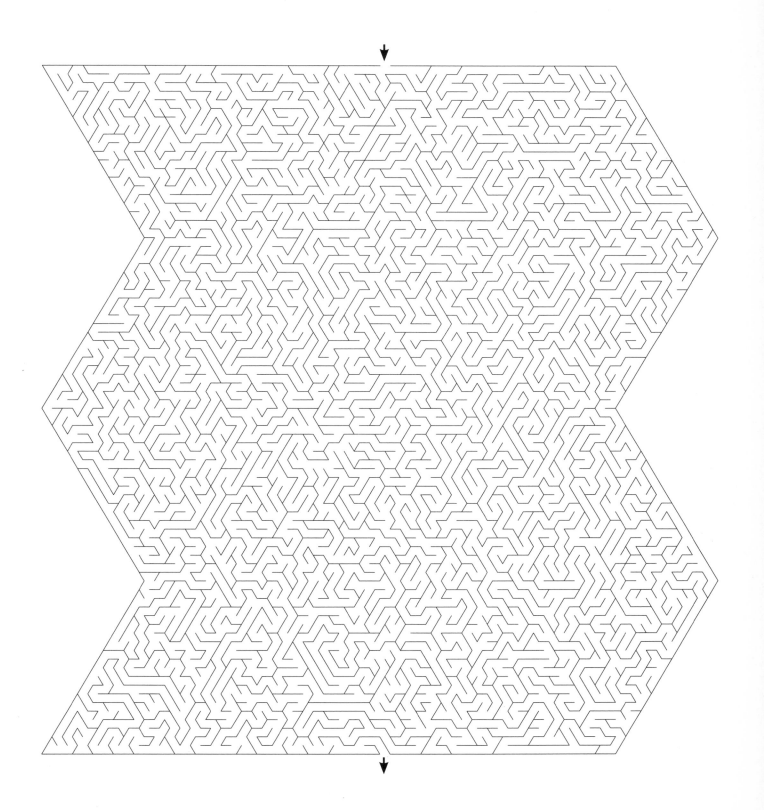

71. CURVING MAZE

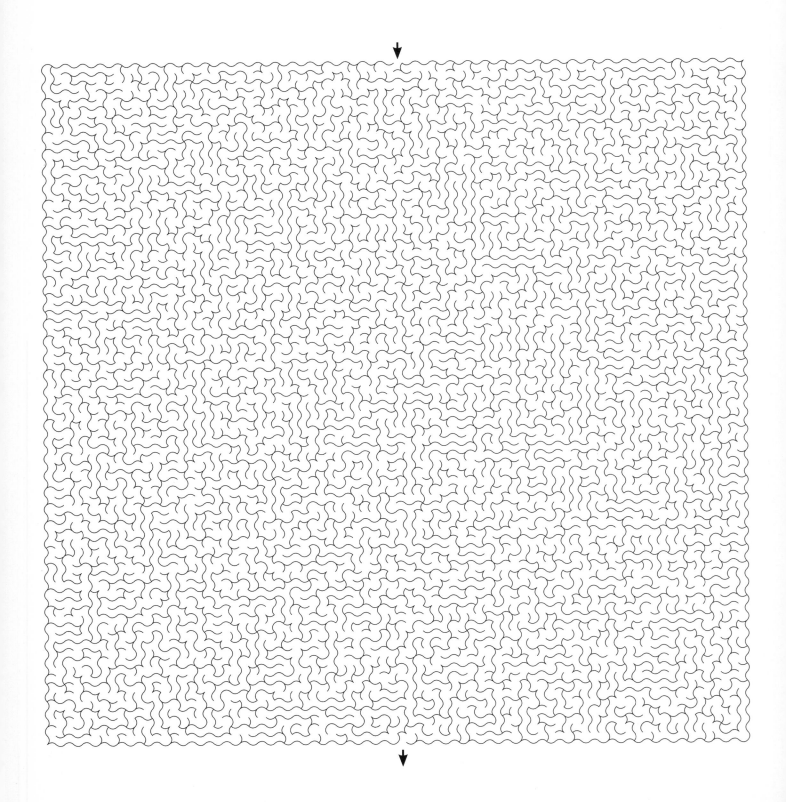

72. BRIDGE MAZE

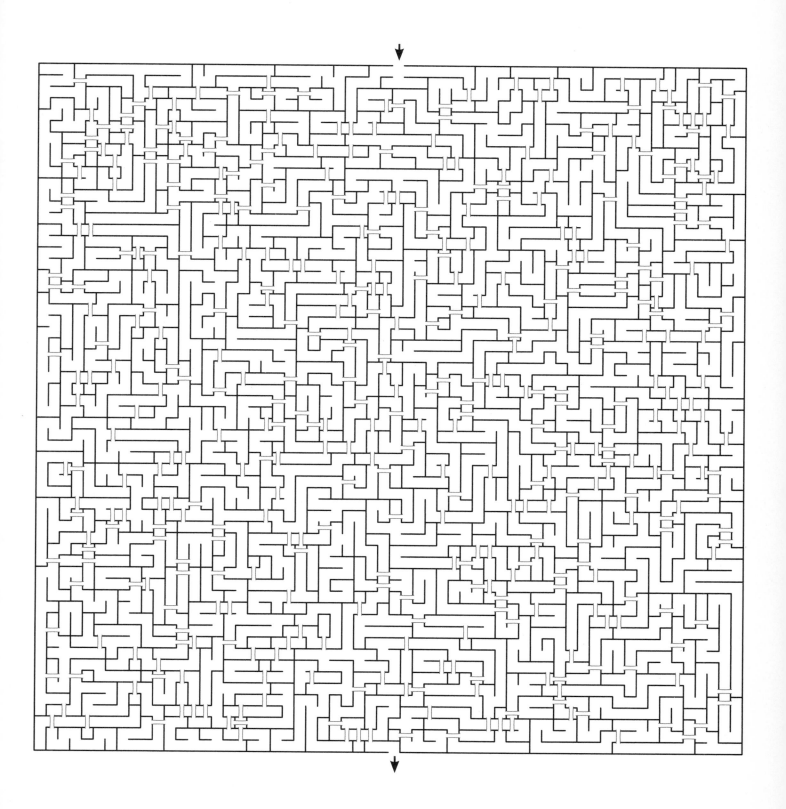

73. CORRIDORS MAZE

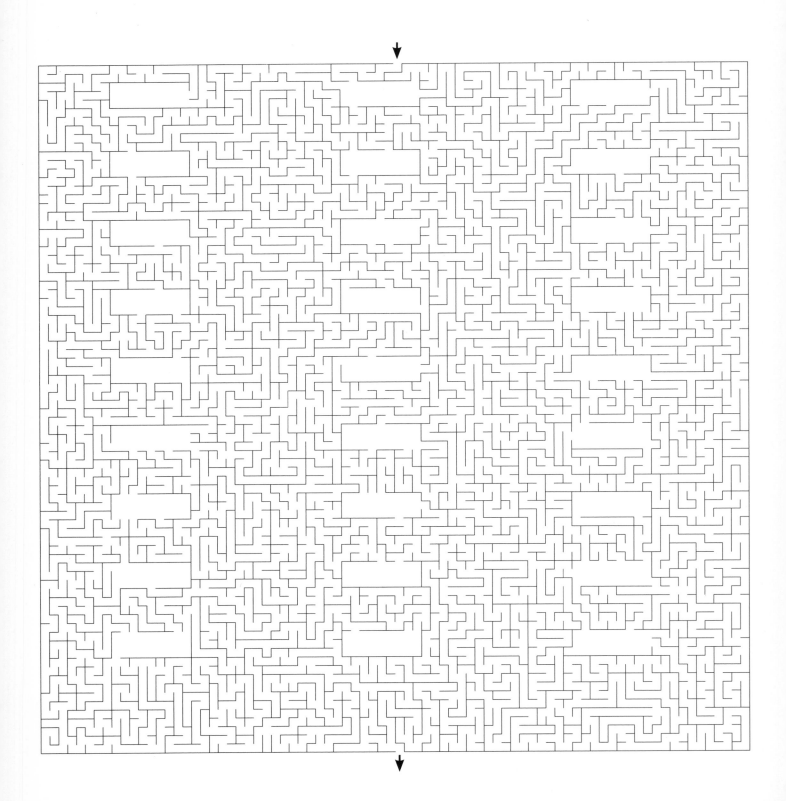

74. OCTAGONAL MAZE

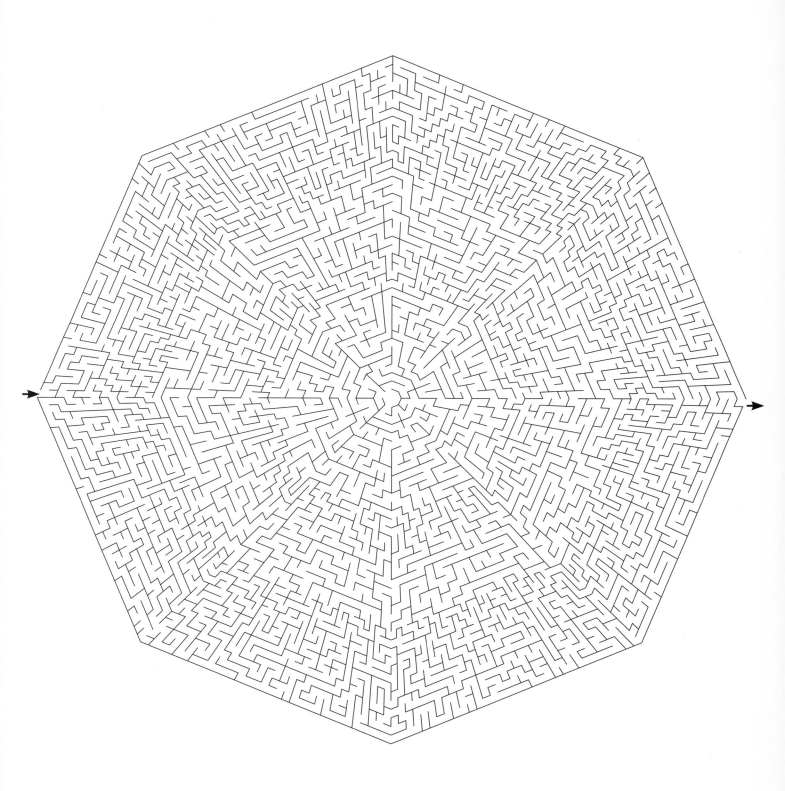

75. WARP MAZE

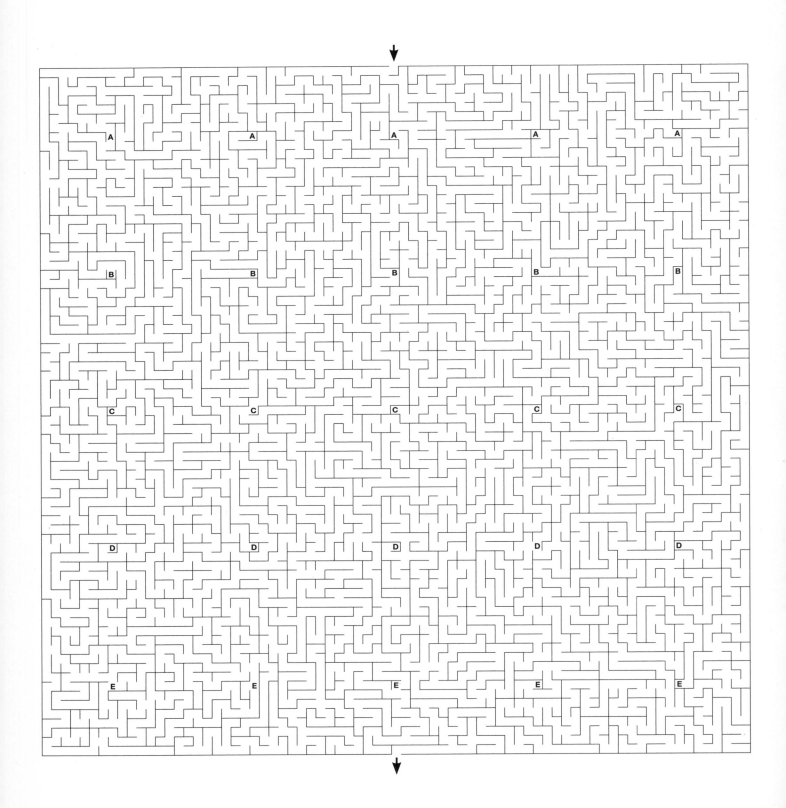

76. TRIANGULAR MAZE

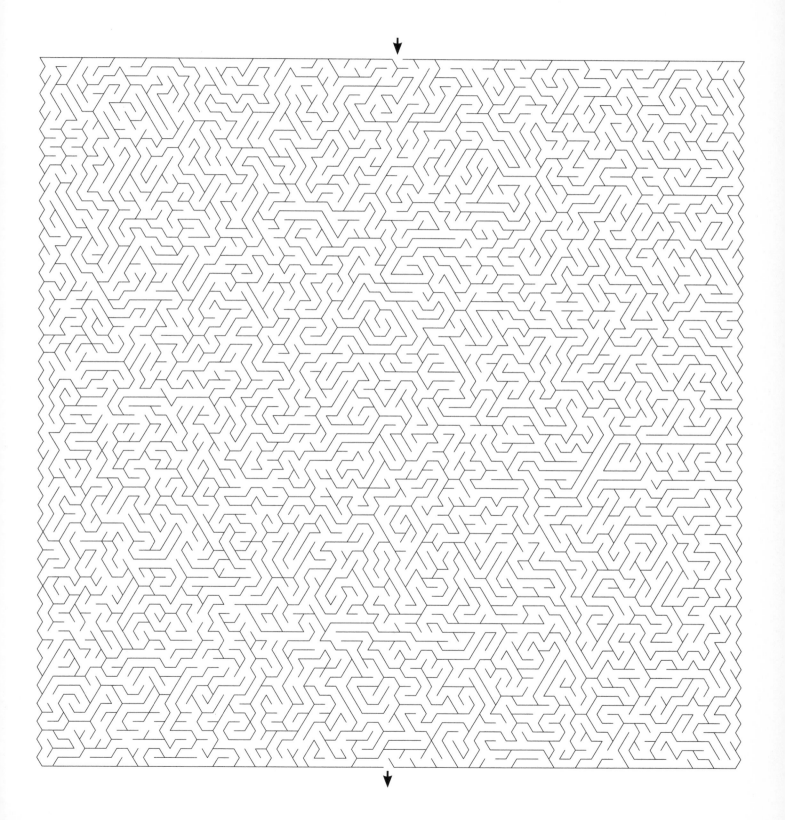

77. CIRCULAR MAZE

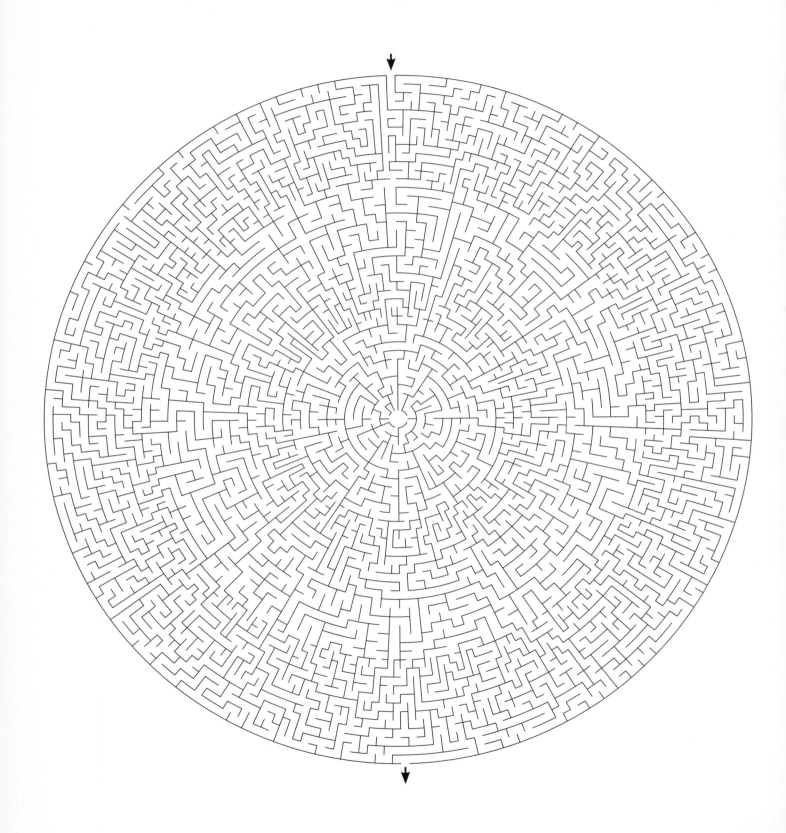

78. ROOMS MAZE

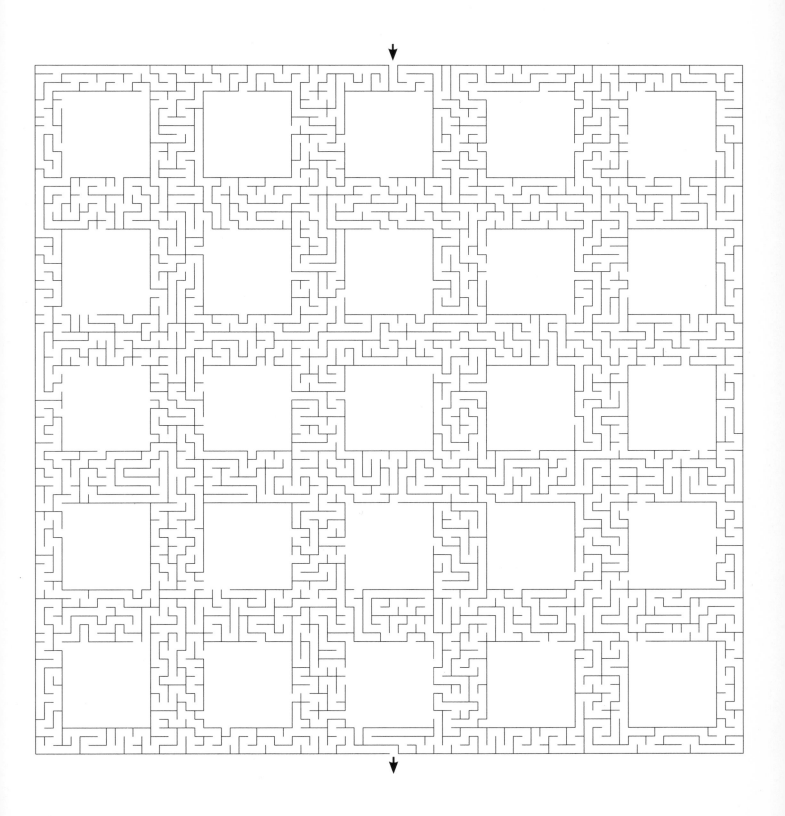

79. MULTI-LEVEL MAZE

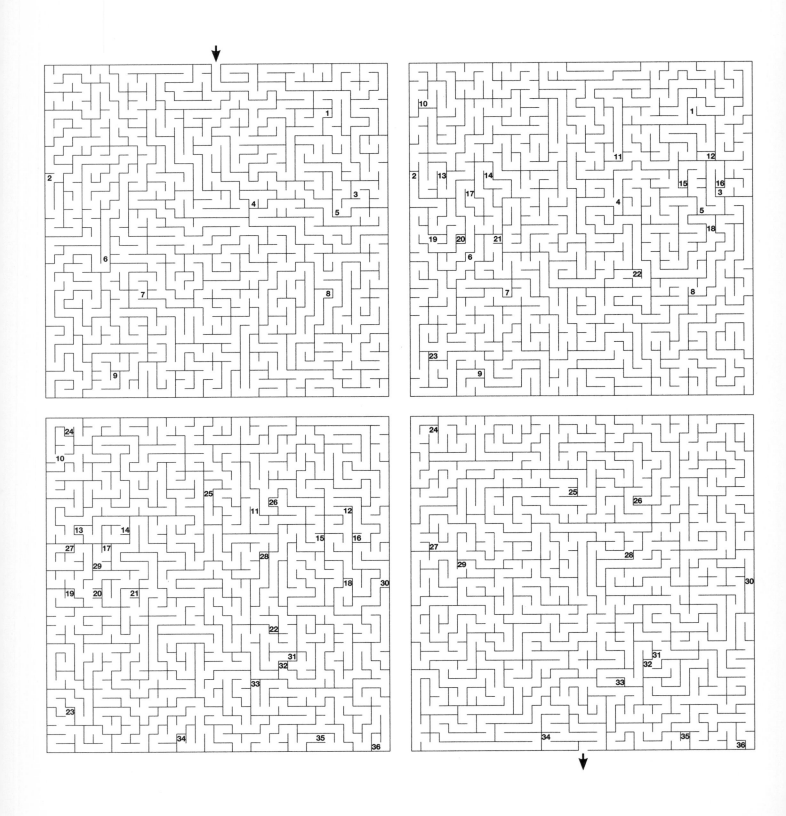

80. BRIDGE MAZE

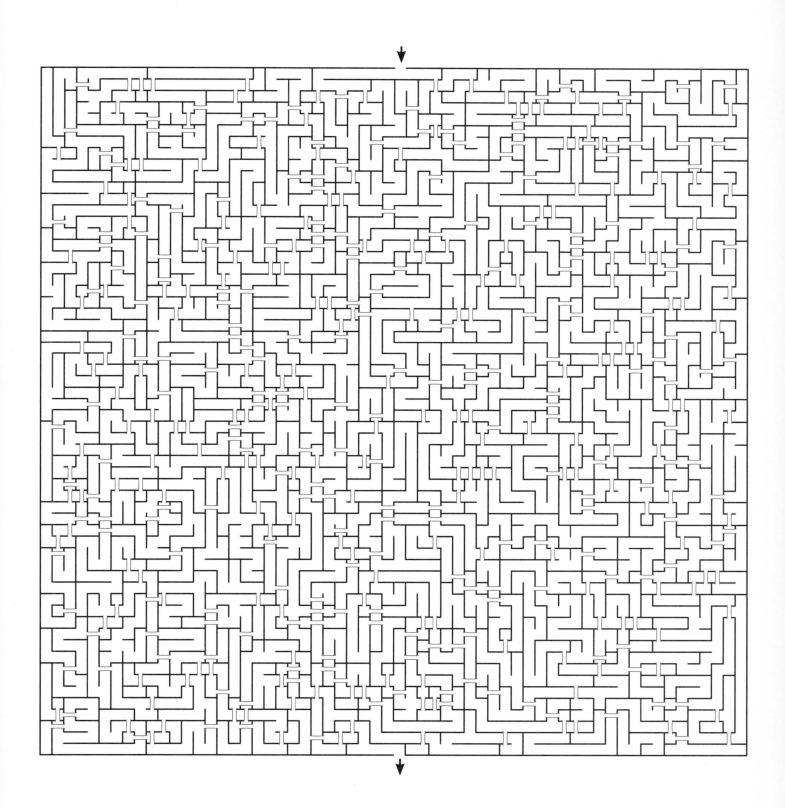

SOLUTIONS

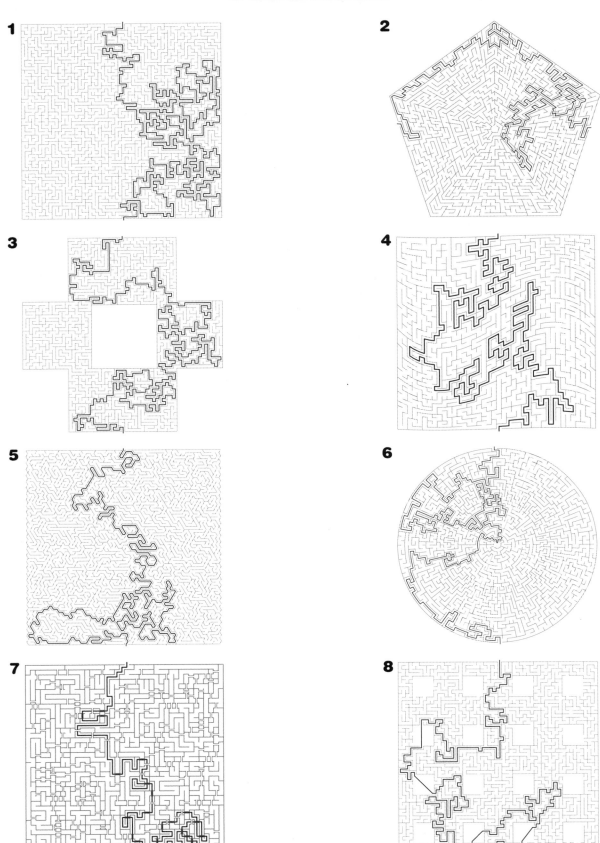

SOLUTIONS

9

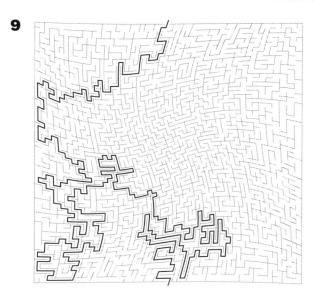

10

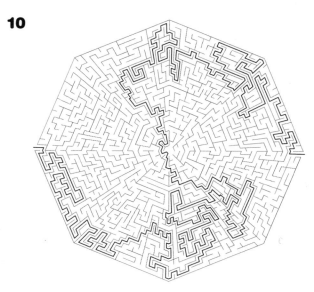

11

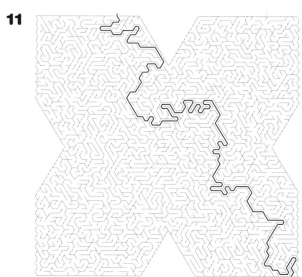

12

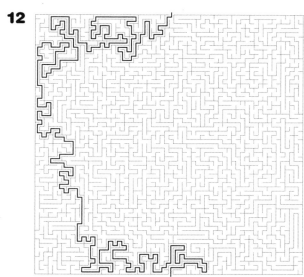

13

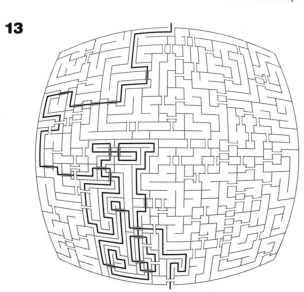

14

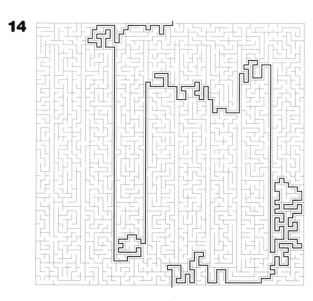

SOLUTIONS

15

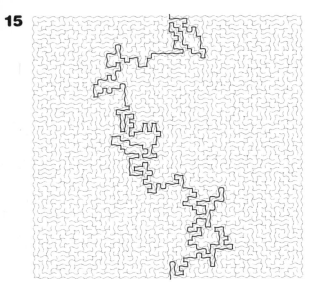

16

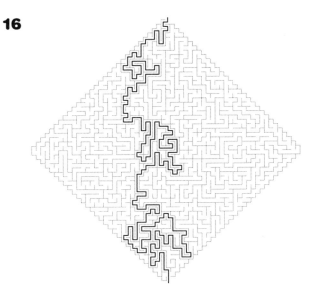

17

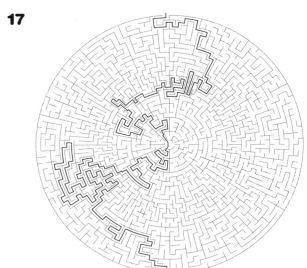

18

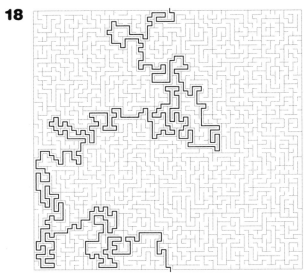

19

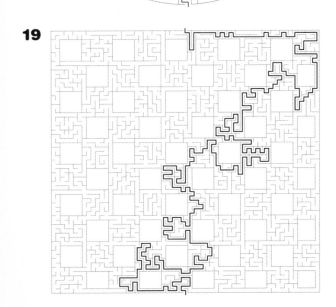

20

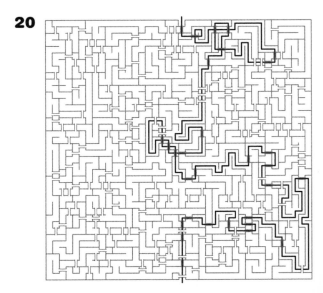

SOLUTIONS

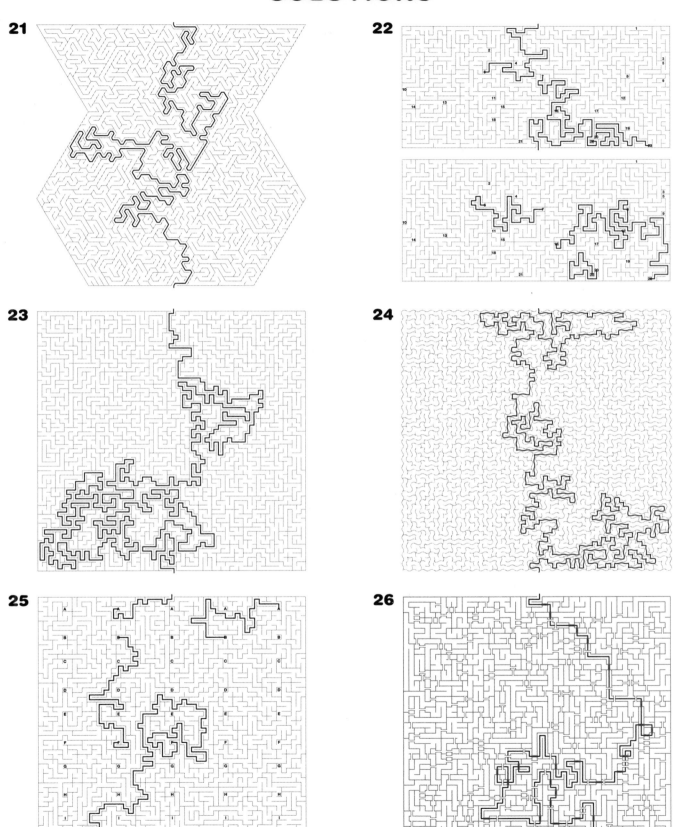

SOLUTIONS

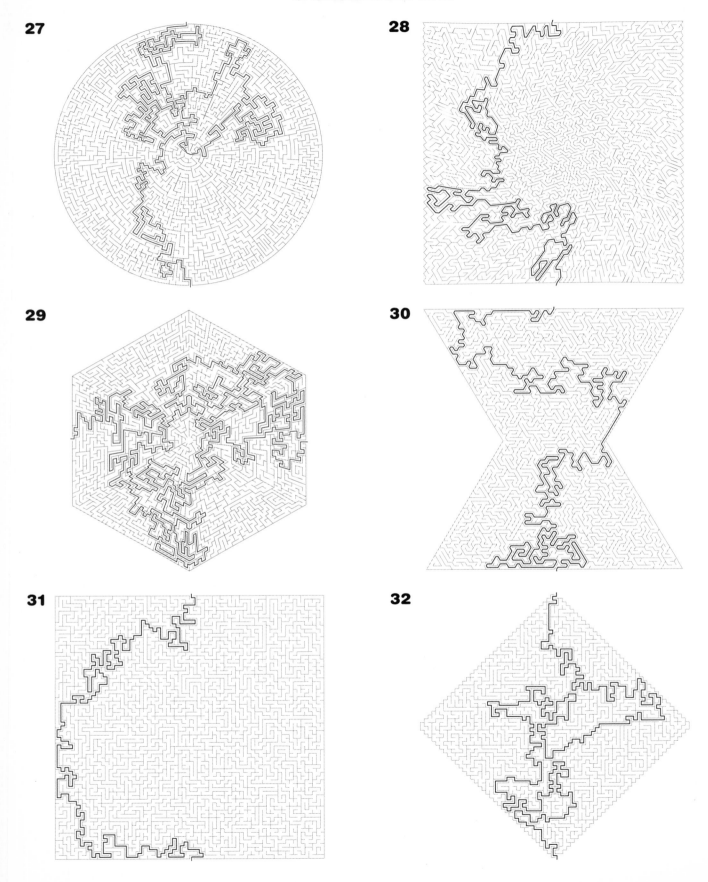

SOLUTIONS

33

34

35

36

37

38

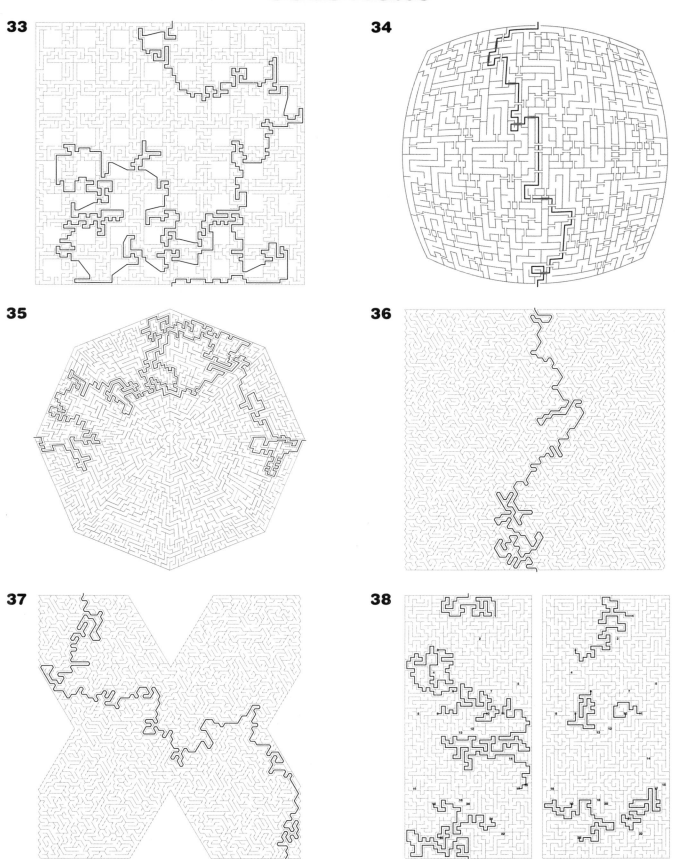

SOLUTIONS

39

40

41

42

43

44

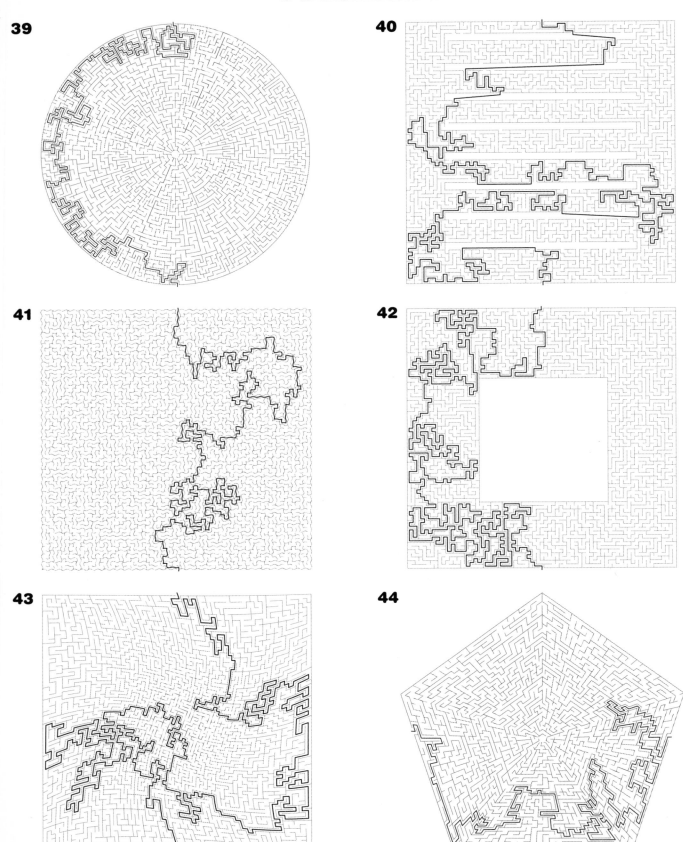

SOLUTIONS

45
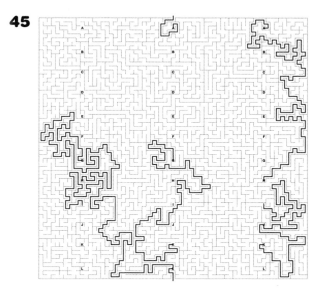

46
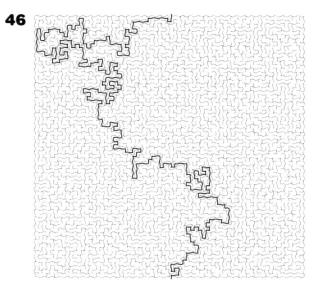

47
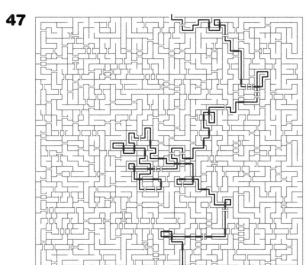

48
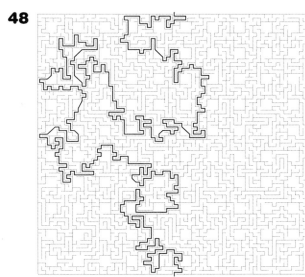

49
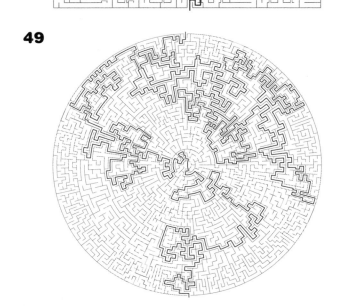

50
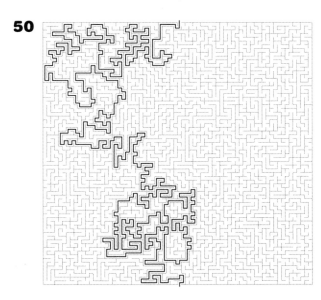

SOLUTIONS

51

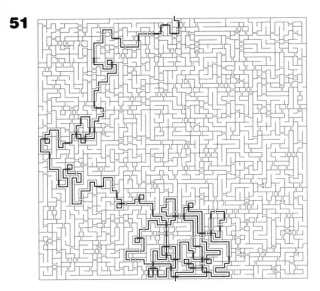

52

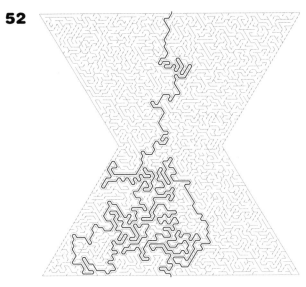

53

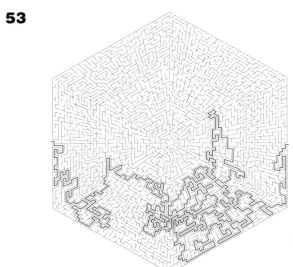

54

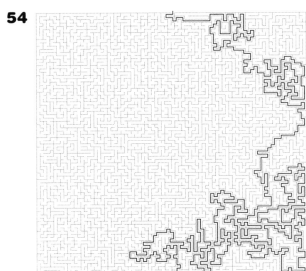

55

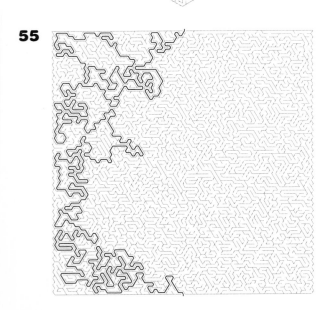

56

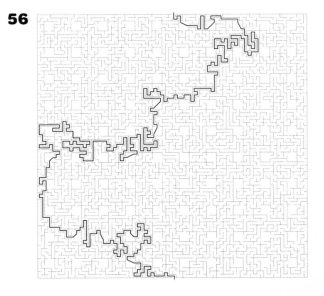

SOLUTIONS

57

58

59

60

61

62

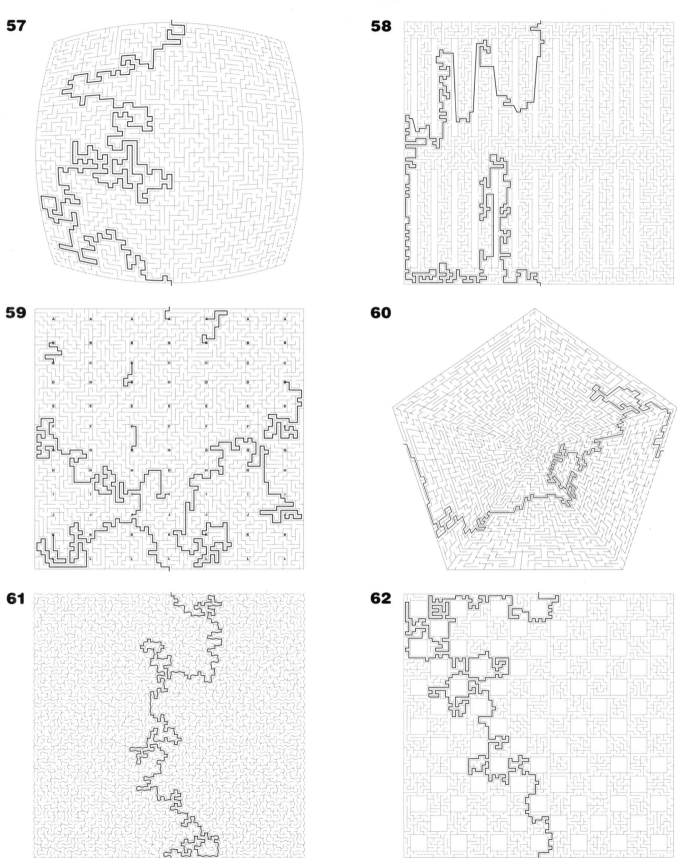

SOLUTIONS

63

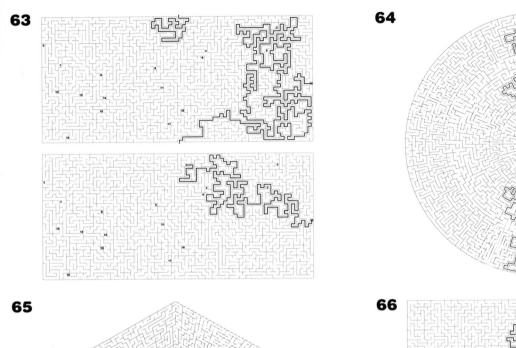

64

65

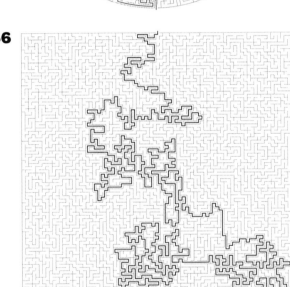

66

67

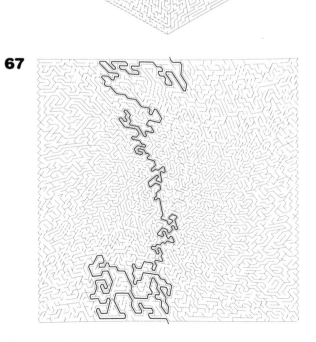

68

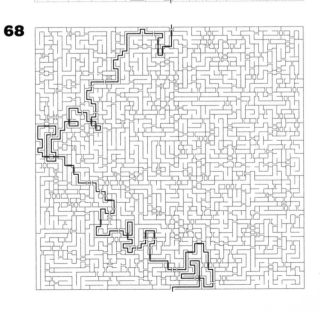

SOLUTIONS

69

70

71

72

73

74

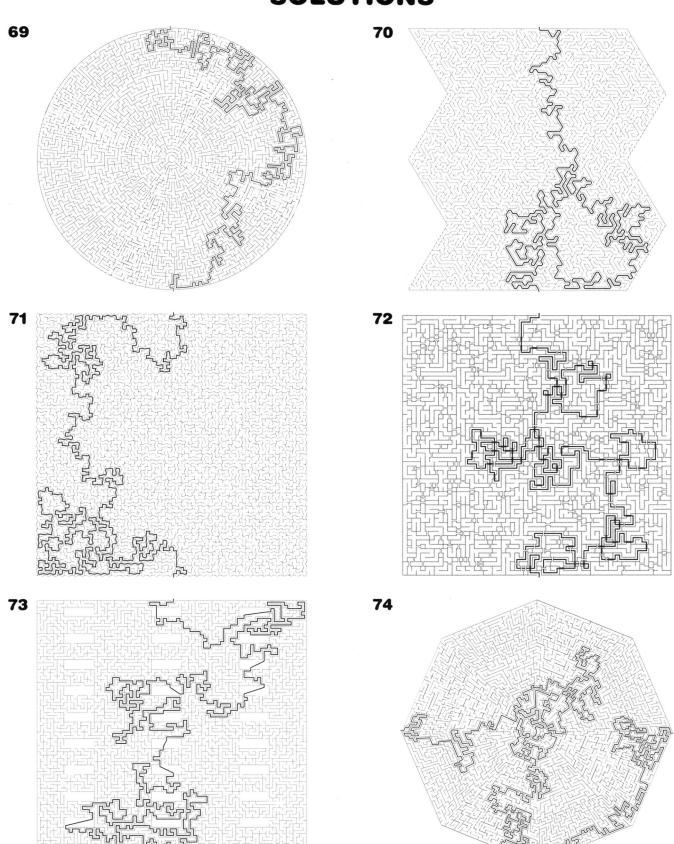

SOLUTIONS

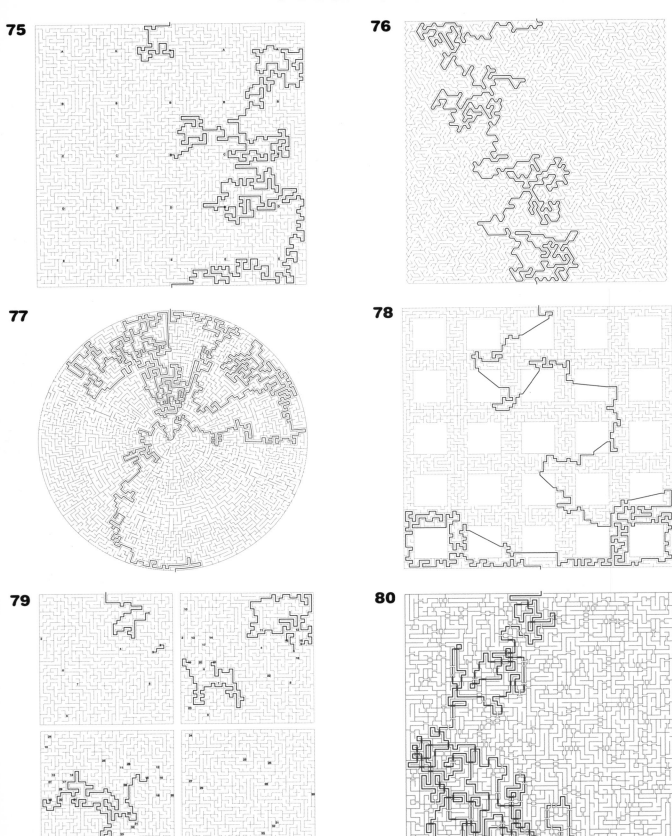